THE EXTREME WEATHER SURVIVAL MANUAL

CONTENTS

OUTDOORLIFE

THE EXTREME WEATHER SURVIVAL MANUAL

DENNIS MERSEREAU

WITH ROBERT F. JAMES AND
THE EDITORS OF *OUTDOOR LIFE*

weldon**owen**

SPRING

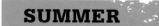

SUMMER

FALL

FROM *OUTDOOR LIFE*

Humans don't share much. As a species, we are solitary keepers. Except for a brief time in college (or the military, or the Burning Man event in Nevada's desert), we keep our own households, separate from the rest of our tribe. Despite every effort of Facebook, we keep our own memories, our own things, even our own histories.

But what we share, often spectacularly and usually with personal anecdote, is the weather. It unites us more than languages or cultures do, and the more extreme the weather, the more it galvanizes those of us who live with it, and through it.

This is a book about the most unifying force on earth: catastrophic weather. But it's only not a worst-case survival manual that may save your life. It's also a lively textbook that will make you smarter. Author Dennis Mersereau is determined to teach you about the weather, and with that education, to better appreciate the awesome power and beauty of the elements behaving badly.

This book will teach you how to read a television weather map, but also how to anticipate the path of a killer tornado. It will teach you which lightning is harmless, and which might light you up like a Roman candle. It will teach you how to minimize the impacts of crippling drought, and how to explain the jet stream and the El Nino effect at your next cocktail party.

Mersereau is the perfect guide to this troubled world of unstable weather. He's a self-described "weather geek" who grew up in the American South, where freak storms and unexpected blizzards were part of the landscape.

Now, Mersereau is one of a new breed of weather nerds who aren't network meteorologists or employed by the National Weather Service, but who enlarge our understanding of the weather as internet bloggers. And he's one of the best, routinely identifying and quashing weather-related nonsense that often goes viral and contributes to our collective misunderstanding of the weather.

This book is the antidote to that sort of crowd-sourced ignorance. It's smart. It's useful. And it's real. Because no matter whether you live in Alabama or Armenia, you will at some point have to deal with flooding, and with drought, with killer storms and with ominous-looking clouds. You'd better know how to drive on black ice, and how to survive in a snowbound car if you go off the road.

There are hundreds of tutorials between these covers that will save your life or enlarge your understanding of our world. Both are useful. Because if you make it through that big storm, you are going to talk about it. You can't help it. You are human, and one of the only things you can't keep to yourself is your experience with our weather.

Andrew McKean
Editor-in-Chief, *Outdoor Life*

INTRODUCTION

Weather is the most spectacularly beautiful and destructive force on Earth. The same atmosphere that can dazzle us with a serene, vivid sunset in one town can simultaneously wipe the neighboring town off the map in a violent fury. Meteorology, or the study of weather, is a fascinating topic that covers almost every aspect of our atmosphere, from the patches of frost on your front lawn to storm systems that stretch across entire continents.

Weather is as terrifying as it is awe-inspiring, and it can take some quick thinking and clever skills to survive the elements. One of the greatest advancements we have made as a civilization is the development of weather forecasting, which has advanced over the years to an incredible degree of accuracy. Every day, tens of thousands of meteorologists around the world provide spot-on forecasts that help people from all walks of life figure out what they should wear or what they need to do to save their lives.

This book will cover most of the major weather phenomena we experience on a daily basis, breaking down each type of weather by the season in which it most commonly occurs. You will learn about blizzards, ice storms, and even the much-feared and misunderstood polar vortex in the Winter chapter, while the Spring chapter holds vital information about severe weather such as tornadoes, hail, and lightning. You will quickly see that weather events are not strictly confined to a specific season—tornadoes can and do occur at any

time of the year in the United States, for instance—but they fit in our seasonal boxes pretty well.

In the Summer chapter we'll talk about hurricanes and floods, as well as heat waves and deadly droughts. And what about Fall? The funny thing about fall is that, well, there's not really much *there* there. The first half is dominated by the last gasps of summer, with oppressive heat and the destructive wildfires that so often follow. The second half is characterized by the ominous sense that, as they say, winter is coming.

We close out the book with some of the wackier side of weather—interesting conspiracies, wild conjectures, and things you probably never even thought to ask—like, do volcanoes cause weird weather?

My goal with this book is to make you fall as much in love with the weather as I have over the years. There is so much more to the weather than fodder for small talk—even the calmest day of blue skies and bright sunshine is exciting if you look just beneath the surface.

001 MEET THE WEATHER

The weather is strange in that it is seen as both personal and impersonal. Each weather event can affect our lives in the most profound ways, yet these deeply personal impacts are not at all unique. The weather plays a formative role in the lives of every person who currently lives, has ever lived, or ever will live, and it will keep doing so until we cease to exist or pack up and move to another planet. Understanding our powerful and fragile atmosphere is important not only because it affects our lives, but also because it's just darn cool. So bear with me while I get really nerdy for a bit.

LEARN THE LANGUAGE It seems elementary, but in order to fully understand the weather, we need to understand the terms used to talk about different weather events. Weather happens at three scales—synoptic, mesoscale, and microscale. Synoptic-scale meteorology deals with large systems such as hurricanes, nor'easters, and fronts—cold, warm, stationary, and so on—that can have an effect on nations or even entire continents. Mesoscale meteorology deals with smaller weather events such as squall lines, clusters of thunderstorms, lake-effect snow, and sea breezes. Microscale meteorology involves weather that occurs on a local basis, such as winds and clouds interacting with individual mountains, cold air draining down into a dip in the terrain, and even dust devils that spin up over a hot parking lot.

KNOW YOUR TERMS One of the most widely employed terms in weather forecasting is "precipitation." Precipitation involves any liquid or ice that falls from the sky: rain, snow, sleet, freezing rain, hail, and graupel. We will get into all of those precipitation processes in due time. Along those lines, we will talk about "severe weather" quite frequently, especially when it comes to springtime. Events such as blizzards and flash floods are certainly good examples of severe weather, but we will use the term to refer to severe thunderstorms, or those thunderstorms that produce damaging winds, large hail, or tornadoes.

002 PREDICT THE FUTURE

All of us have joked about meteorologists flipping a coin to arrive at tomorrow's weather, but the science of meteorology has advanced to the point where today, our forecasts are extremely accurate. In fact, we can now predict major weather events days before they happen, when such precision was almost unthinkable just a few decades ago.

THE BASIC TOOLBOX Meteorologists use a wide array of tools to produce their forecasts. The first step in producing a forecast is to take a look at what's going on in the atmosphere right now, starting with the upper levels (usually around 30,000 feet) and ending with weather at the surface. To begin a forecast, first look at the jet stream, or the fast-flowing river of air in the upper atmosphere. The jet stream is the driving factor for most major weather events. Meteorologists then look at different features in the mid levels of the atmosphere before arriving at the surface, studying data collected by radar sites (to see precipitation) and the thousands of weather stations scattered around the world.

THE CRYSTAL BALL The next step in the forecast process is to use weather models as guidance to help predict where different weather features will form over the next 10 days or so. These complicated computer algorithms aren't the answer—they can often tell an incomplete story—but when good information from weather models is combined with a meteorologist's knowledge and their experience, the result is an excellent forecast.

Does that mean nobody ever gets a little overexcited and predicts a Snowpocalypse! that fizzles? Of course not. But it happens a lot less often than you might think.

003 BECOME A METEOROLOGIST

If your love for weather knows no bounds, you might want to become a meteorologist—but it's no cakewalk. The world's atmosphere is a dynamic, complex machine. To fully understand and predict the weather, you'll need a thorough grounding in math and physics. Majoring in meteorology at a university requires a full load of rigorous calculus and advanced physics courses—so many of these courses, in fact, that many students pursuing a life of forecasting wind up double-majoring or taking up minors in the two subjects. If you're a hardworking student who's up for the challenge, it's well worth the effort.

For those of us who are passionate about the weather but can't do math to save our lives, most meteorology programs offer a minor that provides a solid education into meteorology without any of the in-depth science that requires high-level math and physics. It's a great option if you're looking to learn about the weather while pursuing other fields of study.

004 GET A GOOD MODEL

A weather model is a complex computer algorithm that scientists use to help predict the weather. While they're not the sole tools meteorologists use to create forecasts, models are an integral part of the process. Without weather models, our ability to predict the weather would revert back to the methods used in the mid-twentieth century—making it hard to predict the weather tomorrow, let alone five days in advance.

These advanced models need to know what the weather is doing right now in order to predict what it will do in the future. The computers need to be fed current weather conditions gathered by surface weather stations, weather balloons (as well as some high-flying aircraft) and satellites, along with weather radar. These models are then able to plug all of those current observations into the various algorithms, and then, using climatology (past weather) for guidance, they can help forecasters issue reliable predictions.

There are dozens of weather models available to meteorologists on the Internet. Some of them are provided for free, such as the ones run by the United States government, while others are stuck behind a hefty paywall, such as the model run by the European Centre for Medium-Range Weather Forecasts, often called the ECMWF or "Euro" for short. Each model has its strengths and weaknesses. The United States' Global Forecast System (GFS) weather model is run on a global scale; it's great at handling large-scale features that cover entire countries, but it doesn't do a very good job with small-scale features that only span a couple of counties.

005

READ A WEATHER MAP

Weather maps are omnipresent in modern society. We see them on the television, in our newspapers, and all over the Internet. Understanding how to read a weather map is crucial to understanding how the weather works. The three major parts of a weather map are contours, shading, and symbols.

UNDERSTAND CONTOUR

A contour is a line drawn onto a map that denotes a constant—a constant temperature (an isotherm), a constant pressure (an isobar), a constant amount of precipitation (an isohyet for rain), and so on.

SEE THE SHADING

Contour maps are fairly easy to read, especially when the area in between contours is shaded with a color or pattern. We are the most familiar with shaded contour maps when we look at a day's predicted high temperatures. As a general (and logical!) rule, cooler colors indicate cooler temperatures, and warmer colors indicate warmer temperatures.

DECODE SYMBOLS The

symbols used by meteorologists to denote various conditions don't mean much to the general public, but they're still in widespread use with folks who require advanced weather briefings (such as pilots and sea captains). These symbols are most commonly used on a surface analysis chart, which maps out observations recorded by weather stations. Four dots arranged in a diamond pattern, for example, indicates heavy rain, while two asterisks arranged next to each other indicates light snow. One of the most well-known symbols is an arrow roughly shaped like an "R," denoting a thunderstorm.

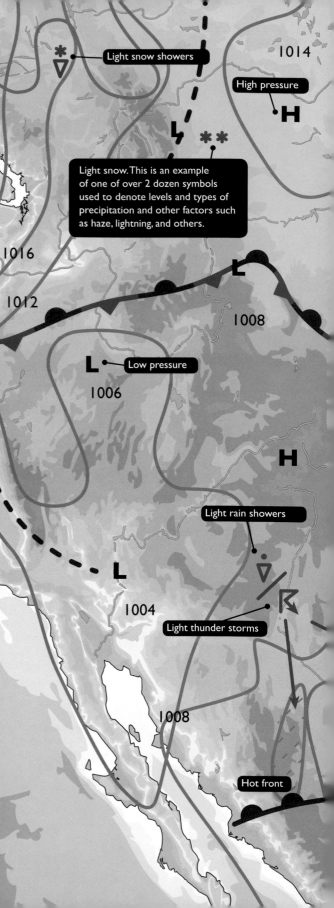

Light snow showers

1014

High pressure

H

Light snow. This is an example of one of over 2 dozen symbols used to denote levels and types of precipitation and other factors such as haze, lightning, and others.

1024

1016

1020

1012

L

1008

L — Low pressure

1006

H

Light rain showers

1004

Light thunder storms

1008

Hot front

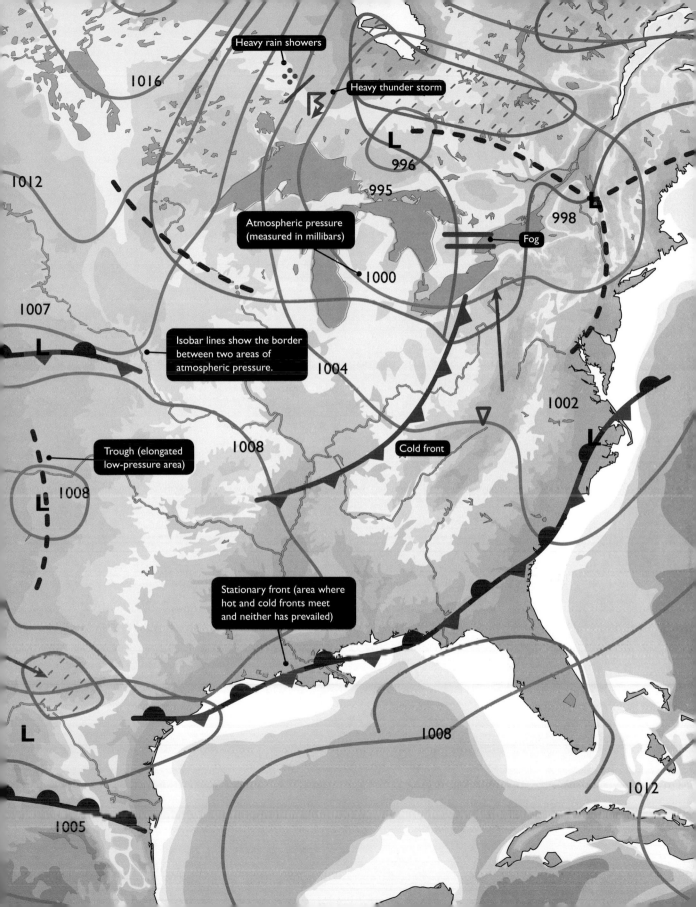

Heavy rain showers

Heavy thunder storm

1016

1012

L
996

995

Atmospheric pressure
(measured in millibars)

998

Fog

1000

1007

Isobar lines show the border
between two areas of
atmospheric pressure.

1004

L

1002

1008

L

Trough (elongated
low-pressure area)

Cold front

1008

L

Stationary front (area where
hot and cold fronts meet
and neither has prevailed)

L

1008

L

1012

1005

006 SURVIVE UNDER PRESSURE

Our atmosphere is heavy. On an average day, the Earth's atmosphere applies 14.7 pounds of force per square inch to every surface at sea level. However, we don't measure the weight of the atmosphere, but rather the pressure it applies on weather instruments called barometers. The average weight of the atmosphere at sea level equates to 29.92 inches of mercury (inHg) or 1013.25 millibars.

MAKE A WAVE Imagine moving your hand through a bathtub full of water with enough force to create a wave that moves from the front of the tub to the back. While the wave is sloshing back and forth, the deepest water in the tub is underneath the crest of the wave, while the shallowest water is found underneath the trough of the wave. High- and low-pressure systems in the atmosphere work in a similar manner. Low pressure occurs when there are fewer air molecules over a particular location, leading to a lower atmospheric weight and thus a lower atmospheric pressure. High pressure occurs when air molecules are densely packed over a particular location, leading to a higher atmospheric weight and a higher corresponding pressure.

RIDE THE RIDGE We're all familiar with those iconic, nearly circular highs and lows, especially intense low-pressure systems like hurricanes or nor'easters. However, most of our weather is created by elongated areas of high and low pressure known as ridges and troughs, respectively. Ridges and troughs can occur in all layers of the atmosphere, from the surface to the level of the jet stream. Ridges of high pressure typically feature warmer-than-normal temperatures and calm weather, while troughs often bring colder-than-normal temperatures and active weather.

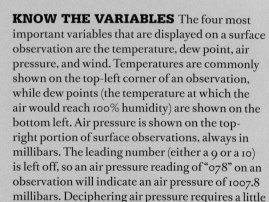

007 READ SURFACE OBSERVATIONS

Surface observations recorded by stations around the world provide some of the most basic weather data available. Records of temperature readings date back hundreds of years—in fact, Thomas Jefferson recorded four temperature readings in Philadelphia on July 4, 1776, the day that the Continental Congress adopted the Declaration of Independence. (It was 76°F at 1:00 PM, if you were wondering.)

ANALYZE THIS Surface observations are usually printed on a map called a "surface analysis" that allows people to quickly get an idea of current conditions across an area. The most complicated surface observations can show up to eighteen variables in one tiny space, which is confusing for even the most seasoned weather buffs.

KNOW THE VARIABLES The four most important variables that are displayed on a surface observation are the temperature, dew point, air pressure, and wind. Temperatures are commonly shown on the top-left corner of an observation, while dew points (the temperature at which the air would reach 100% humidity) are shown on the bottom left. Air pressure is shown on the top-right portion of surface observations, always in millibars. The leading number (either a 9 or a 10) is left off, so an air pressure reading of "078" on an observation will indicate an air pressure of 1007.8 millibars. Deciphering air pressure requires a little bit of critical thinking; for example, the only time that "078" would stand for 907.8 millibars is if the surface observation was taken from the center of a devastating hurricane.

READ THE BARBS Wind barbs are the most recognizable and widely used observation symbols. The barb informs the reader of the speed and direction of the wind at that location. The barb points in the direction from which the wind is blowing; a straight-up wind barb denotes a wind blowing from the north. The spikes and flags extending off of the wind barb denote wind speeds in knots. Long spikes represent 10 knots (11.5 mph), short spikes indicate 5 knots (5.8 mph), and flags represent 50-knot (58 mph) winds.

JOIN THE FRONT LINE

	WHAT IS IT?	WHY DOES IT HAPPEN?	WHAT HAPPENS NEXT?
COLD FRONT	The leading edge of a cold air mass.	Cold air is dense and hugs the ground like a bubble, so cold fronts look like the front of a shoe as they move across the earth. Cold fronts vary in size from a few dozen miles long to an entire continent in length.	Temperatures tend to drop rapidly after a cold front passes by. As a result of the dense air behind them, cold fronts force air to lift, often triggering violent thunderstorms when they collide with a warm, humid air mass.
WARM FRONT	The leading edge of a warm air mass.	Warm air is less dense than cold air, so the leading edge of a warm front passes overhead long before you can detect it at the surface.	Warm fronts tend to create widespread areas of clouds and rain, and during severe weather outbreaks, these fronts can serve as a focus for severe thunderstorms.
STATIONARY FRONT	The boundary between warm and cold air masses that are stalled next to each other.	These fronts can separate dramatically different air masses. For example, in the southeastern United States, cities north of a stationary front could see cool, dry temperatures, while cities south of the front experience warm, humid conditions.	A stationary front will turn into a warm or cold front when one of the air masses begins to move.
OCCLUDED FRONT	The most complicated type of frontal system, where cold and warm interact.	These develop when a cold front overtakes a warm front near the center of a low-pressure system, cutting off (occluding) the warm air from the surface and forcing it to remain aloft.	The point where an occluded front, a cold front, and a warm front meet is known as the "triple point," and the area around the triple point can serve as the trigger for severe thunderstorms.
DRY LINE	A special kind of front that denotes the movement of moisture as opposed to the movement of temperatures.	In general, conditions to the west of a dry line are warm and dry, while conditions to the east of a dry line are warm and moist.	During spring months, these often serve as a focal point for supercell thunderstorms, the most intense type of thunderstorms on Earth.

009 UNDERSTAND PROBABILITY

Discussing probabilities, such as the chance of rain or snow, is a touchy subject in meteorology. People don't like uncertainty; they want their forecasters to definitively say "Yes, it will rain" or "No, it will not," even if the facts don't back it up. Any hint of uncertainty is seen as evasive or even a sign of ignorance about the subject at hand. The latter is actually quite true: we have to use probabilities because predicting the future involves a certain level of ignorance. Unless you're a clairvoyant with your own series of infomercials, nobody can be certain of what will happen in the future until it does happen, and this is very much true in the field of weather forecasting.

PLAY THE PERCENTAGES

Probabilities are a meteorologist's way for them to conveying uncertainty to the public. So, a 40% chance of rain means that there is a chance that it could rain, but forecasters don't have enough evidence to be sure. Probabilities are easier in some cases than others. When a hurricane approaches the coast, it's a pretty safe bet to issue a 100% chance of rain for cities that are in the path of the storm. On the other hand, when you visit Alabama in August, you never know exactly where thunderstorms will spring up and pour for half an hour. The very nature of pop-up summertime thunderstorms makes them virtually unpredictable until they begin to form, so the forecaster's confidence in precipitation is greatly diminished.

PREDICT DISASTERS

The probability of severe weather gets even hairier. The Storm Prediction Center issues forecast probabilities in advance of severe weather in the USA. During the spring months, it's not uncommon to hear forecasters talk about a 10% risk of tornadoes over a certain area. In this case, it means that you'll have a 10% chance of seeing at least one tornado appear within 25 miles of any point in the risk zone. Since tornadoes are far less common than rain or snow, a 10% chance of a tornado means that you need to pay attention to the weather and get ready to go.

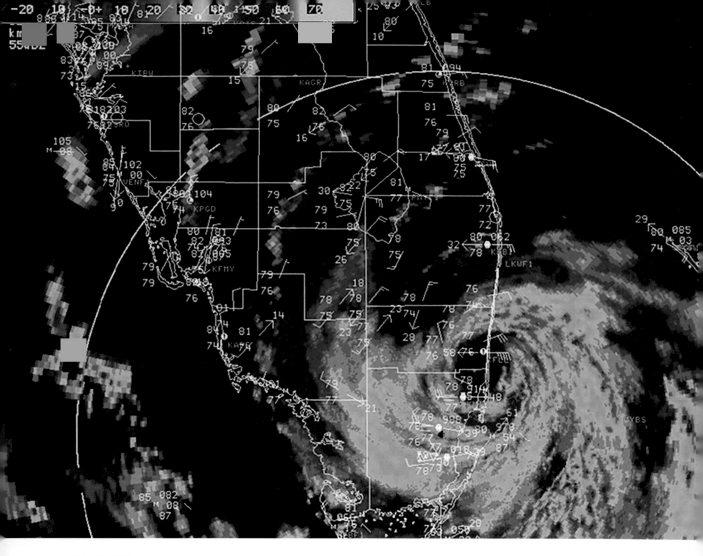

010 INTERPRET WEATHER RADAR

First discovered during the intense military operations of World War II, the use of radar technology to monitor precipitation is now an integral part of weather reports around the world. Weather radar is a lifesaving tool that helps users answer questions ranging from "Do I need an umbrella?" to "Do I need to run for shelter?"

FEEL THE PULSE Weather radar works by sending out pulses of microwave radiation into the atmosphere. If there is precipitation present, the radiation will bounce off of it and then return to the radar site. Computers then calculate the intensity and distance of the precipitation. Government-run weather radar sites located in the U.S. were updated in the 1990s to include Doppler capabilities, which allow the devices to detect the speed and direction of the precipitation as well, giving us the ability to see winds within a storm. This is crucial in detecting events like tornadoes and damaging winds.

READ THE RAINBOW When an information agency wants to display radar imagery on television or online, most media outlets employ a standard scale to help viewers understand what they're seeing. Cooler colors such as blue and green are used to represent lighter precipitation, while the warmer colors ranging from orange to red are used to indicate heavy precipitation, such as flooding rains or large hail in a severe thunderstorm. Some outlets like the Weather Channel are even able to incorporate temperature data into radar imagery to show viewers where rain, snow, sleet, and freezing rain are falling at any given time.

KEEP IT LOCAL There is one important caveat to remember when you're looking at radar imagery. Due to the curvature of the Earth, the radar's beam of radiation gets higher off of the ground the farther it gets from the radar site, so precipitation far away from the radar site is going to be a few thousand feet off the ground. Always try to look at a radar image close to where you live, or you might not see the whole picture.

011 GAZE AT EARTH FROM ABOVE WITH SATELLITES

One of the most iconic images in world history is the Blue Marble, or the gorgeous photo of Earth captured by the crew of Apollo 17 as they headed to the moon in 1972. It's awe-inspiring to gaze at our pale blue dot from above, and thanks to technology, we can see images of our planet beamed back to the ground in real time by dozens of weather satellites parked in orbit a few hundred miles above our heads.

Meteorologists have used weather satellites since the space race as a way to keep up with weather systems around the world. While they're capable of a lot more than cloud gazing, the three most commonly used satellite products available to the public—visible, infrared, and water vapor—are all used to track clouds and moisture.

Visible satellite imagery is the easiest to decipher, as it's simply a snapshot of the Earth as it would appear to orbiting astronauts or alien passersby. Infrared satellite imagery uses infrared light to determine the temperature of the clouds, which aids in determining how tall clouds are (higher clouds are colder). Infrared satellite images use a color-coded scale to show temperatures—white colors show warmer/lower clouds, and vivid red, purple, and even black show extremely tall clouds in the bitter cold of the upper levels. Water vapor imagery detects the amount of moisture in the atmosphere in the mid levels, around 10,000 feet above the surface. Like infrared, water vapor is also depicted using a color-coded scale; warm colors show dry air, and cool colors show moist air.

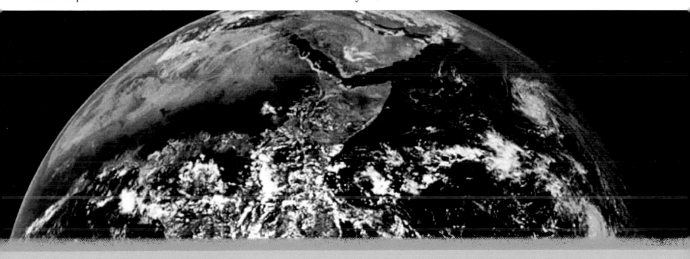

012 LEARN FROM A BALLOON

When we look at a weather report, most people only care about temperature, moisture, and wind here at the surface. However, we've actually known since the 1700s that studying these variables in the sky above is just as important. One of the United States' first weather observers, John Jeffries, is widely credited as the first person to take weather observations using a balloon, back in 1784.

Today, the process is a little more advanced (though decidedly less cool) than launching weather cowboys into the sky, thermometer in hand. Hundreds of large, latex weather balloons are launched around the world twice a day to take temperature, pressure, moisture, and wind data between the surface and the top of the troposphere, or the bottom layer of the atmosphere in which almost all weather occurs. Each balloon contains an instrument package called a "rawinsonde" that records these variables and transmits them back to meteorologists on the ground.

The data collected by weather balloons can be visualized in a graphic called a "SKEW-T" chart (see item #29) that basically traces the temperature and dew point of the atmosphere along the balloon's path, along with the winds from the surface to higher than the jet stream. Looking at these variables allows us to make forecasts such as determining if a location will see snow or rain, as well as showing us thunderstorm development.

013

LEARN TO EASILY IDENTIFY CLOUDS

All those clouds you see drifting by overhead are differently shaped and sized for some very important reasons. Here's how to tell them apart, and understand what spotting each type might mean for the weather.

CUMULUS

The most recognizable of all clouds. Puffy and resembling huge balls of cotton, cumulus form when pockets of warm air at the surface rise up through cooler air above, a process called convection. Small patches of harmless cumulus are commonly called "fair-weather clouds," but they can grow much more ominous.

CUMULONIMBUS

Towering storm clouds that result from strong instability, or the rapid rising of warm, moist air called an updraft. Cumulonimbus clouds are synonymous with thunderstorms. The vast majority of these thunderstorms are not all that severe, but a small percentage can still produce flooding rains, damaging winds, large hailstones, and even tornadoes.

ALTOSTRATUS

Forming in the mid levels of the atmosphere, altostratus clouds appear as a thin, milky layer that covers the sky like a veil. The sun and moon appear blurry through altostratus clouds, but they are not completely obscured.

ALTOCUMULUS
The mid-level cousin to regular ol' cumulus, altocumulus clouds form as a result of convection. Altocumulus can form in large sheets that stretch off beyond the horizon, often resulting in magnificent textured sunsets.

STRATUS
This is the most boring type of cloud. As opposed to the small-scale, focused lift that produces cumulus, stratus are the result of large-scale lifting and are associated with those dreary, rainy days. Picture the most depressing, uniformly gray sky you can think of, and that's a stratus cloud.

CIRRUS
Composed of ice crystals that form in the higher levels of the atmosphere, cirrus clouds are associated with generally fair weather. Thanks to strong winds in the upper atmosphere, cirrus are thin and wispy, appearing as if they were created with a paintbrush.

UNDULATUS ASPERATUS
The first new cloud formation identified since 1951, undulatus asperatus ("turbulent undulation") has been described as "menacing [and] roiling." This cloud type has lately been submitted to the World Meteorological Association for consideration. It has not yet been confirmed whether the new cloud will be added to the official Cloud Atlas in 2015, but it seems likely.

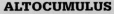

014 TRUST YOUR GOVERNMENT (OR SOMEONE ELSE'S)

Most governments around the world operate their own agencies dedicated to predicting and monitoring the weather. These special departments aren't there just to provide weather information to the public—weather forecasting is very important for commercial and military activities. Governments have a vested interest in keeping abreast of any weather conditions that could impact their country's ability to prosper. Major flooding or exceptional droughts can devastate agricultural industries, causing billions of dollars in lost crops, to say nothing of the resulting economic hardship and food shortages. Severe thunderstorms and extreme winter weather can delay or cancel planes, trains, trucks, and even ships, causing financial losses and supply chain issues, and throwing a wrench in the plans of millions of people.

AGENCIES IN THE U.S. The most well-known of governmental weather agencies in the world is the National Weather Service (NWS) in the United States, which falls under the control of the National Oceanic and Atmospheric Administration, or NOAA. The NWS is further subdivided into several specialized agencies, most notably the Storm Prediction Center, which handles severe thunderstorms, and the National Hurricane Center, and local offices across the country.

GLOBAL RESOURCES Contrary to whatever we Americans may think, the United States actually isn't the center of the universe. The United Kingdom's Met Office, Environment Canada, MétéoFrance, the Japan Meteorological Agency, and countless other bureaus throughout the world—even North Korea's Hydrometeorological Service—keep an eye on the skies to make sure that no system, no matter how remote, goes unwatched.

BRINGING IT ALL TOGETHER With so many government agencies operating independently, it can be very difficult to maintain and enforce a set of standards. The United Nations agency that deals with meteorology around the world is aptly called the World Meteorological Organization, or the WMO. One of the WMO's most visible responsibilities is to maintain the worldwide lists of tropical cyclone names. Each of the seven tropical basins around the world has its own list of rotating names used to keep track of tropical cyclones; each list is populated with names submitted by countries that surround each basin. When a storm has caused an especially large amount of death and destruction on landfall, the WMO is also responsible for retiring that storm's name and replacing it with a new one.

015 STOCK YOUR HOME

Chances are, we've all experienced a power outage at one point or another. Usually, it's in the middle of our favorite television program or movie, and the response is one of disappointment, sometimes profane, at the interruption. The reality, however, is that most households are unprepared for losing that power for anything longer than a couple of hours. What happens if, on top of no power, the water also runs out? What are you going to do when the freezer thaws out after 24 hours without electricity? What if you have special medical needs? Are you prepared? Home survival isn't that different from wilderness survival. The benefit is that you don't have to carry everything you'll need. And you also can benefit from some household hacks to turn run-of-the-mill products into life-saving materials:

①

②

③

1. WATER Have a weeks' worth for you and your family (1 gallon per person per day—and don't forget about pets!). If bottled water runs out, remember there's water in the tanks of your toilets. If you're lucky and you have advance notice that your water supply might be jeopardized, fill up your bathtub with water so you have extra.

2. FOOD You can survive a surprisingly long time without food, so food is less of a concern. Stock up on easy dried foods to get you through the worst of it. Canned foods that don't need heating are a good idea, as are pre-packaged, high-calorie snacks. Rather than storing rice and beans in their original bags, which can rip, transfer them into 2-liter bottles for easy storing.

3. MEDICAL SUPPLIES When you're making your at-home medical kit, think big. This isn't some portable

kit that fits in your pack or the trunk of your car. Spend time and a little extra cash to cover all the potential medical issues you might encounter. You also should prepare to deal with your prescription medical needs. Insulin, for example, needs to be kept refrigerated.

4. RADIO A battery-powered radio is sufficient for a few days if you need to monitor emergency services; you might want one that includes NOAA weather bands in the U.S.. Be sure you have plenty of batteries, too. A hand-powered radio is even better. Current models also include cell-phone chargers—a potential life-saver. If you need AA batteries and only have AAA, wad up aluminum foil between the battery and the connections.

5. CANDLES AND MATCHES If you're out of candles, raid the kids' room for crayons. A single crayon

will burn for half an hour. Or you can put a wick in a can of vegetable shortening for a long-lasting candle.

6. DUCT TAPE Because you can do virtually anything with it. Really.

7. SHELTER AND WARMTH Chances are, you already have enough blankets in your house to help keep your family warm. But it's never a bad idea to have some survival blankets as part of your emergency preparedness kit. It's also a good idea to keep some rain tarps handy, just in case you end up with a hole in your roof or some other damage to your home that ends up exposing you to the elements.

016 PREPARE YOUR HOME

Don't forget that a house also is part of your survival kit, so keep it ready. Putting plywood under your bed or against the closet walls will help you shore up windows or doors without having to go outside. Additional door and window locks will help keep you secure. And motion-activated lights or cameras can help you see what's going on outside while you're safe and secure.

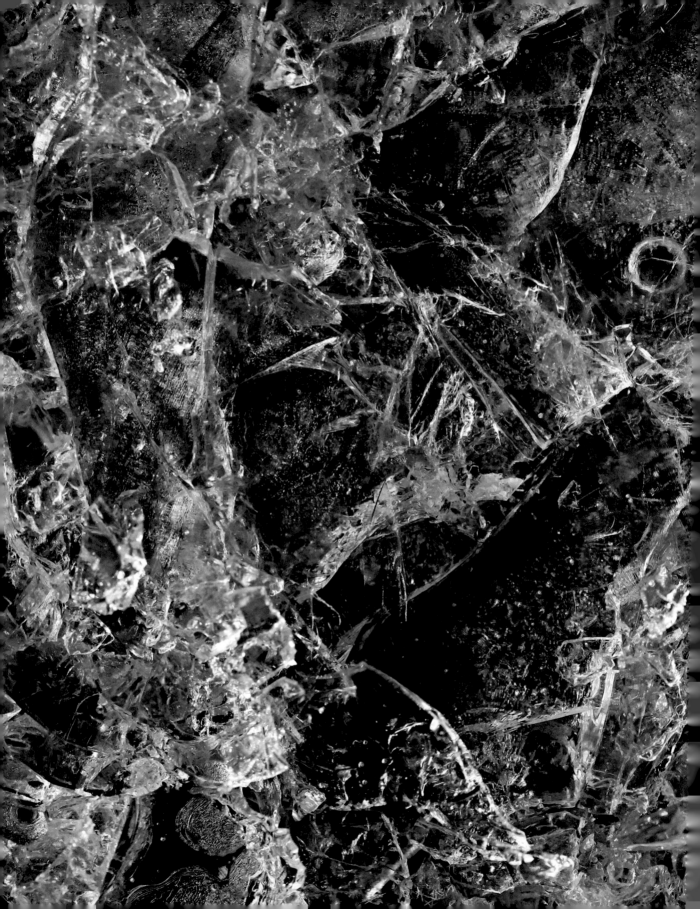

❄ WINTER

Imagine looking out your window at a wintry scene filled with barren, frost-tipped trees keeping watch over blanketed lawns specked with snowmen. The mental image in your head will create a feeling of serenity, joy, fear, depression, or raging anger—winter manages to evoke people's full range of emotions, often all in one day. In short, winter is truly a gorgeous pain in the butt.

The reason for the astronomical season is one of the first things they teach us in school. The Earth is tilted on its axis, so for a quarter of the year, the Northern Hemisphere directly faces the sun, and for another quarter of the year, it's the Southern Hemisphere's turn to get blasted by the direct rays of our very own star. Winters in the Northern Hemisphere are more brutal than those for our friends below the Equator, because the northern half of the globe has more land than ocean. Land heats up and cools down much faster than water, so the Arctic-bearing hemisphere can get extremely cold for many months of the year.

Winter is more than just piles of snow building up around the edges of strip-mall parking lots. We can see five major types of precipitation—rain, snow, sleet, freezing rain, and graupel—during the winter, all of which have different characteristics, different risks, and require very different weather conditions to form. If you live in the northern United States or Canada, you might be surprised to learn just how hard it is to get wintry weather to develop in much of the world in the middle and lower latitudes. Just a one- or two-degree

difference in the air a few thousand feet up above our heads can spell the difference between a cold rain, an icy disaster, or a snowy wonderland.

Precipitation is often the most advertised feature of winter weather, but it's not the only player in the game. Exposure to bitterly cold temperatures is a major concern, especially when they have reached record levels. As many as 500 people die every year in the United States as a result of hypothermia, or a dangerous drop in one's body temperature caused by prolonged unprotected exposure to cold weather. During those hot, steamy southern summers, residents love telling outsiders, "It's not the heat that gets you. It's the humidity." Well, the same holds true for the winter: it's not always the cold that gets you, it's the wind.

Winter is an exciting, versatile season that can bring joy to a kid's face and strike fear in the hearts of weary commuters. Almost everyone is affected by some extreme winter weather at some point, so it's important to know what it is and how to survive whatever the season can throw at you.

017 KNOW WHAT'S FALLING ON YOU

Precipitation is one of those terms that seems pretty easy to understand. That's rain, right? Well, yes and no. It's rain ... and a lot more. Here's a handy primer on wet stuff that falls from the sky. Why do you need to know this? Well, the gap between rain and sleet doesn't seem like a big deal—but one day, your life might depend on knowing the difference.

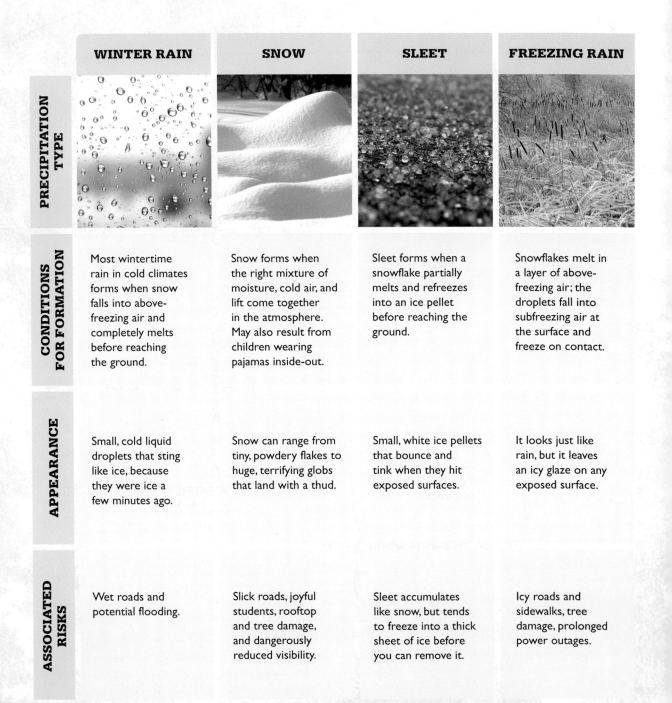

	WINTER RAIN	SNOW	SLEET	FREEZING RAIN
CONDITIONS FOR FORMATION	Most wintertime rain in cold climates forms when snow falls into above-freezing air and completely melts before reaching the ground.	Snow forms when the right mixture of moisture, cold air, and lift come together in the atmosphere. May also result from children wearing pajamas inside-out.	Sleet forms when a snowflake partially melts and refreezes into an ice pellet before reaching the ground.	Snowflakes melt in a layer of above-freezing air; the droplets fall into subfreezing air at the surface and freeze on contact.
APPEARANCE	Small, cold liquid droplets that sting like ice, because they were ice a few minutes ago.	Snow can range from tiny, powdery flakes to huge, terrifying globs that land with a thud.	Small, white ice pellets that bounce and tink when they hit exposed surfaces.	It looks just like rain, but it leaves an icy glaze on any exposed surface.
ASSOCIATED RISKS	Wet roads and potential flooding.	Slick roads, joyful students, rooftop and tree damage, and dangerously reduced visibility.	Sleet accumulates like snow, but tends to freeze into a thick sheet of ice before you can remove it.	Icy roads and sidewalks, tree damage, prolonged power outages.

018
UNDERSTAND WIND CHILL

You don't need a weatherman to know which way the wind blows, but you might want to listen to him when he tells you that it'll be windy when it's bitterly cold.

CHILLY AIR An air temperature of 0°F is cold enough, but when you factor in a 25 MPH wind, the weather is downright unbearable unless you're wrapped up from head to toe. One common measure we use during the winter is the "wind chill," or how cold the combination of frigid temperatures and stiff winds feel on exposed skin.

LOSING THE BUBBLE On a calm, cold morning, your skin is partially protected by a bubble of warmth radiating from your body. When the wind starts blowing, it can remove this layer of warm air, exposing your skin directly to the elements. The cold, dry wind accelerates your body's heat loss by evaporating moisture from your skin, causing your surface temperature to further plummet.

FREEZING COLD If the air is cold enough, your skin can begin to freeze, leading to a serious medical condition called frostbite. The effects of frostbite can range from mild redness and a burning and stinging sensation to complete skin cell death, which requires expert intervention (and in the most extreme cases, may even need amputation).

CHART IT OUT The National Weather Service uses a formula developed by scientists to determine wind chill. Using this tool, it's pretty easy to tell what the wind chill will be. In the above example, a temperature of 0°F and a 25 MPH wind would produce a dangerous wind chill of -24°F; frostbite would develop in just 30 minutes.

GRAUPEL	FREEZING FOG
Graupel forms when water vapor deposits ice on snowflakes.	Fog that develops when air temperatures are below freezing.
Graupel has the look and feel of Dippin' Dots. It tinks like sleet but falls apart like snow.	Freezing fog can be deceiving because it looks like regular fog, but it's far more dangerous.
Graupel has the same impacts and risks as snow.	Reduced visibility, a thin glaze of ice on exposed surfaces, accumulating ice in some conditions.

WEATHER WORLD RECORDS
FASTEST TEMPERATURE DROP

If you're averse to wild temperature swings, avoid western South Dakota. Way back in January 1943, the Black Hills town of Spearfish smashed the world record for the fastest temperature drop ever measured. On January 22, the temperature rose 49 degrees, from -4°F to 45°F in just 2 minutes! A couple of hours later it plunged from 54°F back down to -4°F in 27 minutes.

019 DON'T GET LOST

Finding your way can be a problem in snowy conditions and in featureless terrain. If you're short on navigational equipment but need to journey away from camp or car, you can use these techniques to blaze your own trail across any landscape.

LEAVE SIGNS As you traverse forests or boulder fields, use something to mark your travel direction on prominent trees and rocks. During emergencies, high impact marking (like chopping arrows into tree bark or chipping rock) may be a necessary method. During lower levels of distress, a simple piece of black charcoal from your campfire can be used to draw arrows or write messages on trees, rocks and other surfaces. Always make your marks at eye level so they won't be missed (by you or by rescuers!).

STACK IT UP A cone of tall sticks, a pile of rocks, or even a snowman can be placed in open areas to indicate the trail at a distance or to signal any other information. Arrows and other signals made of sticks and stones lying on the ground can be used for pathfinding, but a light snow can cover them easily, leaving you stranded.

FLY THE FLAG Strips of colorful fabric or other material can be used as an excellent trail marker in brushy areas and woodland terrain. Consider carrying plastic survey tape so you don't have to end up ripping up your nice red flannel shirt! Choose bright unnatural colors like hot pink or day-glow purple. Hang small strips at eye level, within view of the last marker, to make a clear trail.

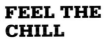

020 FEEL THE CHILL

As we have discussed previously in item 18, wind chill is no joke. A given temperature might be chilly but not dangerous with no wind, but it can become downright deadly when the wind picks up. The faster the wind, the more heat is carried away, and the faster frostbite can set in. Take a look at this handy chart below, to help you visualize what that oft-cited wind- chill factor actually means for your survival.

	Temperature (°F)																	
Calm	40	35	30	25	20	15	10	5	0	-5	-10	-15	-20	-25	-30	-35	-40	-45
5	36	31	25	19	13	7	1	-5	-11	-16	-22	-28	-34	-40	-46	-52	-57	-63
10	34	27	21	15	9	3	-4	-10	-16	-22	-28	-35	-41	-47	-53	-59	-66	-72
15	32	25	19	13	6	0	-7	-13	-19	-26	-32	-39	-45	-51	-58	-64	-71	-77
20	30	24	17	11	4	-2	-9	-15	-22	-29	-35	-42	-48	-55	-61	-68	-74	-81
25	29	23	16	9	3	-4	-11	-17	-24	-31	-37	-44	-51	-58	-64	-71	-78	-84
30	28	22	15	8	1	-5	-12	-19	-26	-33	-39	-46	-53	-60	-67	-73	-80	-87
35	28	21	14	7	0	-7	-14	-21	-27	-34	-41	-48	-55	-62	-69	-76	-82	-89
40	27	20	13	6	-1	-8	-15	-22	-29	-36	-43	-50	-57	-64	-71	-78	-84	-91
45	26	19	12	5	-2	-9	-16	-23	-30	-37	-44	-51	-58	-65	-72	-79	-86	-93
50	26	19	12	4	-3	-10	-17	-24	-31	-38	-45	-52	-60	-67	-74	-81	-88	-95
55	25	18	11	4	-3	-11	-18	-25	-32	-39	-46	-54	-61	-68	-75	-82	-89	-97
60	25	17	10	3	-4	-11	-19	-26	-33	-40	-48	-55	-62	-69	-76	-84	-91	-98

Wind (mph)

Frostbite Times   30 minutes   10 minutes   5 minutes

021 BUILD A SNOW CAVE

So you're stranded outside on a slope and there aren't many shelter options. If all else fails, you can dig yourself a snow cave to stay warm though a frigid night.

STEP 1 Find a spot with deep snow, preferably on a hillside so you can dig straight in. Start off with a low entrance just large enough for you to crawl inside.

STEP 2 After penetrating about 2 feet into the snow, start carving upward to create a dome 4 to 5 feet tall and 6 feet wide.

STEP 3 Against the back wall, shape a sleeping bench 2 feet up from the floor. Poke a small hole in the roof beside the door as an air vent.

STEP 4 Crawl in, cover the entrance with a snow block, then heat the interior with a single candle.

022

TREAT FROSTBITE

What if you ignored all of our warnings and now you're frostbitten? Your best option is to seek medical help. However, if you're snowbound, here's how to stave off disaster, by which we mean losing your fingers or toes. Never rub frostbitten skin, as you can destroy cells and make it worse.

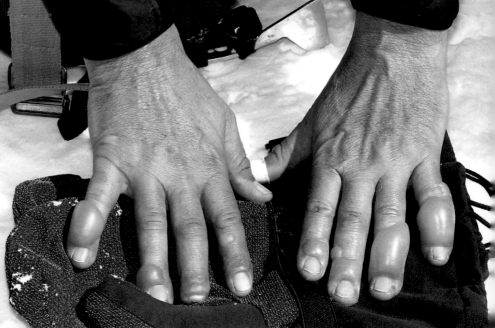

STEP 1 Get out of the cold. If you'll be continuing to expose your frozen flesh to freezing temperatures, don't treat the frostbite until you've gotten to safety.

STEP 2 Remove any jewelry in case you develop any swelling.

STEP 3 Put the affected area into a bath of body-temperature water. Refresh the water frequently as it cools to keep the water at a steady temperature.

STEP 4 If water isn't available, use body heat to treat mild cases of frostbite. But don't position the victim near a heater or an open fire: If there's nerve damage, he or she may not feel tissue begin to burn.

STEP 5 Dress the injury in sterile bandages, wrapping each affected digit individually.

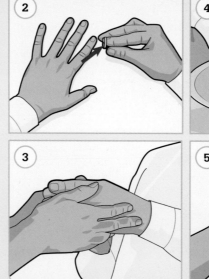

023 PROTECT YOURSELF FROM BITTERLY COLD WINDS

The best way to guard against dangerously cold weather is to make sure that you cover every inch of exposed skin before you go outside. Sure, it's uncomfortable to walk around feeling like a marshmallow person or inept movie criminal because you've got on so many clothes, but it's better to feel and look stupid than lose a chunk of your skin in the name of vanity.

In a perfect world, everyone would have the will to throw on a balaclava, gloves, and a heavy coat before venturing into the frozen tundra (or down to the store), and the money to buy the right gear. Sadly, our world is far from perfect, and it's hard to cover every single bit of your body when it's cold. So, that means that many of us

will still have to deal with exposed faces as we go about our lives in the frigid air. Standing in a bus shelter or behind a wall will help protect you from the wind, and turning your back to the wind as a last resort is a useful (and symbolic!) way to stave off your skin's frosty demise.

Don't forget your kids, either. Children are especially vulnerable to cold weather injuries. Many school districts will delay or cancel classes when extreme cold is in the forecast, but some superintendents are determined to make kids risk injury and tough it out like they had to in the old days. If this is the case, make sure your kids are bundled up, and keep an eye on them until they get in the building or on the bus, if possible.

024 IDENTIFY A COLDQUAKE

If you hear a loud, house-shaking boom on a cold January morning, it might not be your town's biannual oil-train derailment, but something a lot cooler and weirder (and less horrifying). On very rare occasions, some parts of the world can experience a phenomenon that's known as a cryoseism, a small, earthquake-like jolt that results from water seeping into the bedrock and freezing during a cold snap. Water expands when it freezes, so just as the vast majority of earthquakes are caused by tension along a fault line, the ice can create an enormous amount of stress on the rock beneath the earth.

If the tension grows too great, the rock will crack or snap, resulting in a loud noise and possibly a small tremor. Cryoseisms rarely cause property damage, but they can be jarring, especially if you don't know what caused it.

025 KEEP YOUR HOME SAFE

When the temperature plummets, first make sure your kids and pets are safe. Then turn your attention to those valuable inanimate objects—your home and car.

ENHANCE HOME SAFETY

Structures both new and old can sustain serious damage during a brutal cold snap. Plumbing is the most vulnerable part of a structure; water expands when it freezes, and the pressure of ice building up in a pipe can cause it to burst. Allowing faucets, spigots, and even sprinkler systems to drip in a cold snap can help prevent pipes from bursting. It can be pretty annoying to listen to the faucet drip all night, but it's better than shelling out thousands of bucks to repair broken pipes and water damage.

KEEP THE CAR RUNNING

Your car needs some love, too. If you manage to get your car started on a bitter morning, make sure you let it run for a couple of minutes before you get on the road. The oil in your engine is already a viscous, syrupy fluid, and it gets even thicker when it's extremely cold outside. Allowing your car to run for a minute or two will allow the oil to move through the engine and prevent the damage you could cause if you just start up and head out.

026 KEEP ANIMALS AND PLANTS ALIVE

When the forecast calls for an especially frosty period of Arctic air, it's not just humans who can suffer. Be sure that critters and other living things are protected as well.

ANIMALS Frigid weather can pose a serious threat to both pets and livestock. Animals can develop hypothermia and frostbite from cold and wind just like humans; leaving these lovable creatures exposed to the elements for very long could cost them their lives. It's not just dogs and cats you should worry about, either. A freak blizzard in South Dakota in October 2013 left at least 14,000 cattle dead as a result of heavy snow and cold temperatures. One way to help livestock is to be sure they have extra food and water.

PLANTS Many of your plants can require even more careful attention than humans or animals in cold weather. We laugh at Floridians for freaking out when temperatures drop, but cold weather can result in millions of dollars in lost crops. Pay attention to frost and freeze alerts issued by your local weather agency. Covering your plants up or bringing them indoors during cold weather (especially in the early and late stages of winter) can help them survive.

027 KNOW WHAT MAKES COLD SNAPS COLDER

Whether it's the water cycle, the life cycle, a unicycle, or the time cycle, everyone loves a good cycle. One of the ugliest cycles we encounter as we hurtle through the cosmos is the feedback cycle. The weather can create some pretty nasty feedback cycles, most notably during cold snaps.

Before we had artificial cooling in refrigerators, our grandparents had to use an icebox, which used a large block of ice to keep food from spoiling. The ice chilled the air directly above it through conduction, and the entire box would cool down to near-freezing after a couple of hours with the door closed.

The atmosphere works in a similar manner when there's ice and snow on the ground. These substances can act just like ice in an icebox by preventing the atmosphere from warming up to its full potential. The snow's white, reflective surface keeps solar radiation from absorbing into the ground, reducing the sun's ability to warm the air at the surface. The lack of absorbed solar radiation—combined with the chilling effects of the snow itself—can keep temperatures much colder than they would have gotten with bare ground. The snow-induced cooling can help the snow stick around longer, creating a feedback cycle of cold air.

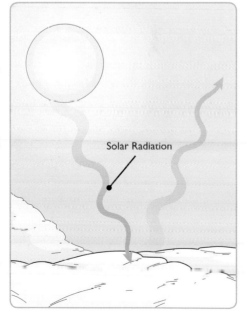

Solar Radiation

028 KNOW YOUR STORMS

What exactly is a "storm," anyway? Four inches of snow in Yellowknife, Northwest Territories, Canada, is just a regular Tuesday afternoon. But that same four inches of snow in Mobile, Alabama, would shut down the city for days. Yellowknifers would just laugh if you called that paltry snowfall a "storm," while Mobilians would be talking about it for decades.

In general, a winter storm is an organized area of precipitation that drops rain, snow, sleet, or freezing rain over a widespread area. Wintry precipitation is strange because it's the same everywhere—the snow in Calgary is the same as the snow in Moscow—but its consequences depend on what residents are used to seeing each year. The impact of winter weather on a region of the world always varies according to that region's ability to mentally and physically deal with snow and ice. Take that into consideration when thinking about winter survival.

Snow is the easiest to manage, because we can shove it to the side and get on with our lives after a day or two. Ice is much harder to deal with, because you can barely make it out your front door without slipping and crashing to the ground.

DENNIS DEBUNKS:
IT DOESN'T SNOW IN FLORIDA

We love to think that the Sunshine State is immune to the white doom, but it can and does snow in Florida from time to time. Strong winter storms can drop several inches of snow across the northern parts of the state. It even snowed in Miami one fateful day: January 19, 1977, is the only day in recorded history that it snowed in typically tropical southeastern Florida.

029 READ A SKEW-T CHART

SKEW-T charts are extremely useful when you want to know what kind of wintry precipitation will fall during a storm. Just a small layer of temperatures one or two degrees above freezing will melt a snowflake and turn a snowy scene into an icy hellscape strewn with downed trees and power lines. Understanding these diagrams requires you to identify five major features, which reflect data gathered by weather balloons (see item 12).

ISOBARS The horizontal lines are isobars, lines of constant air pressure, measured in millibars. The air pressure at ground level changes based on weather systems and the balloon's launch altitude. The jet stream is usually between 200 and 300 millibars.

ISOTHERMS Those diagonal lines that stretch from the bottom left to top right are isotherms, or lines of constant temperature, always measured in Celsius. The 0°C isotherm is the freezing line.

TEMPERATURE The red trace from the bottom to the top of the diagram charts the atmosphere's air temperature as recorded by the weather balloon. The air temperature line is usually drawn in red, but on black-and-white SKEW-T charts, the temperature trace is the line on the right.

DEW POINT The green trace charts the dew point, the temperature at which the air reaches 100% humidity, as measured by the balloon. When the green and red lines are far apart, this means dry air; the two lines come close together when the balloon travels through a region of moist air. The dew point line is always to the left of the temperature line.

WIND BARBS These triangles always appear to the right of a SKEW-T chart, and they correspond to the pressure altitudes. Wind barbs work the same as they would on a surface observation, showing the direction from which the wind blows, with speeds in knots.

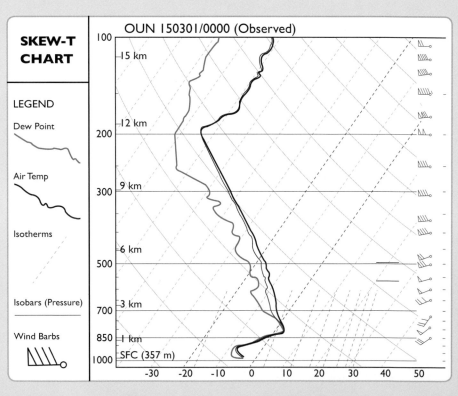

EXTREME WEATHER HISTORY:
THE STORM OF THE CENTURY

We don't name winter storms as we do with hurricanes, but some of the worst storms in history grow nicknames by legend alone. Whether it's the Knickerbocker Blizzard of 1922 or the President's Day Blizzard of 2003, each storm creates a legend that lasts for generations. However, there is one winter storm in history with no peers. It stands alone for its reach and long-lasting effects, and it is known by the only name that fits its fury: "The Storm of the Century."

A low-pressure system developed off the coast of Texas on March 11, 1993, and then explosively intensified as it moved toward Florida the following day. The storm strengthened from virtually nothing to the equivalent of a weak hurricane in just one day, producing a 12-foot storm surge on the western coast of Florida. A powerful line of thunderstorms developed south of the storm along its cold front, destroying thousands of homes and leaving more than 50 people dead across Florida and Cuba.

The snowy side of the storm remains unrivaled today. The size and strength of the nor'easter dragged temperatures down into the teens and even produced several inches of snowfall as far south as the northern Gulf Coast. Birmingham, Alabama, saw its largest snowstorm on record, with 13 inches of snow and a low of 2°F the following morning. Several feet of snow fell on most major cities along the East Coast, and some towns in the Appalachian Mountains saw nearly 4 feet by the end of the storm.

The Storm of the Century is an incredible example of nature's power, and one of the most intense nor'easters ever recorded. Weather geeks may salivate at the thought of another storm of this magnitude, but it caused hundreds of deaths and left behind billions of dollars in damages. It is to our benefit that this kind of a storm is a once-in-a-lifetime occurrence.

030 UNDERSTAND WHY IT SNOWS

The sky is full of floating particles too small for our eyes to see. We can see some of them in high concentrations—dust blowing in the wind, pollen on cars, smoke from a fire, even salt from the ocean—but for the most part, the particles are so widely dispersed in the atmosphere that we can hardly detect them until they make us sneeze. All these flying impurities serve as the catalyst for the development of all precipitation, including snow.

Water vapor requires a small impurity in the air known as a "condensation nucleus" around which to collect and begin forming a raindrop or snowflake. If air temperature is far below freezing, the water vapor won't just condense around the nucleus, but will rather deposit as ice instead, going straight from water vapor to an ice crystal form. The ice crystal that forms on the particle collects more water vapor through deposition, and it then begins to grow into a snowflake.

031 KNOW YOUR SNOW

There are dozens of varieties of snowflakes that can fall, each requiring slightly different set of atmospheric conditions in order to form. Temperatures that are too cold or too warm will cause snowflakes to develop in the shape of plates, cylinders, and needles. The type of snowflake we're most familiar with is called a dendrite.

Dendritic snowflakes are those that develop with a beautiful, complex system of radiating branches—so complex, in fact, that the old cliché "no two snowflakes are exactly alike" is more than likely the truth. Prime conditions to allow dendritic snowflakes to form in the atmosphere arise when the temperatures in the clouds are between -12 °C and -18 °C, a range which meteorologists like to call the "snow growth region." These snowflakes produce the best chance of a pretty, accumulating snowfall.

The amount of snow that falls is determined by something called the rain-to-snow ratio. You might have heard weather nerds talking about 10 inches of snow falling for every inch of rain that would have fallen if it were warmer, but the ratio can differ wildly depending on conditions. When temperatures are very cold, like we usually see in the northern United States and Canada, snow falls in the form of small, powdery flakes. This dry snow has a high ratio, sometimes up to thirty-to-one. On the other hand, marginally cold, very moist air can produce a heavy, wet snow with ratios as low as eight-to-one.

Every once in a while during any of the low-ratio events, you'll see exceptionally large snowflakes that land with a soft thud when they hit the ground. These are dendritic snowflakes that partially melt and stick together as they fall. You could see three or four flakes clumped together, making it look like it's snowing in globs rather than flakes.

032

MEASURE SNOWFALL

Want to brag about how much snow fell in your town last night? What you had to slog through to get to work? How tough could it be, right?

GET IT RIGHT The thing is, there's a little more to it than just sticking a ruler in a snowdrift and then writing down the first number you see. Snow doesn't accumulate evenly on all surfaces. Materials such as concrete or asphalt can retain heat longer than nearby surfaces, so snow accumulation is almost always lower on roads and sidewalks than on the grass a foot away. Measuring snow on the grass isn't the best route, either, because the cushioning effect of the grass and soil might add an extra inch to your totals.

USE A BOARD The best tool for measuring snow is an extremely advanced tool that's called a snow board—a small block of plywood or Styrofoam that's painted white and placed in an open area away from obstructions or disturbances. An untouched deck or wooden railing works just as well in a pinch. Using a snow board will allow the snow to accumulate without having to worry about residual heat or the inflated snow totals you would find on grass.

HURRY UP You will need to measure snow immediately after the last flake falls to minimize the effects of compaction. Snow on the ground can compact several inches in a matter of hours after the snow stops. If the snow drifted because of the wind, take several measurements around the area and average them together to arrive at the snow total.

WEATHER WORLD RECORDS
COLDEST TEMPERATURE ON EARTH

Penguins are hardy, surviving the brutal weather in Antarctica while remaining some of the cutest creatures to waddle the Earth. But even the might of the penguins was challenged on July 21, 1983, when the record for the coldest temperature ever recorded on Earth was set at Antarctica's Vostok Station. The scientific camp's weather station recorded a brisk low temperature of -128.6°F.

033 PREVENT HYPOTHERMIA

Hypothermia is no joke, and it's easy for even a healthy person to fall prey to it while outside during freezing winter weather. A drop in core temperature of as little as 4 degrees can be fatal, and it's likely you won't even see it coming. One of the first lines of defense your body uses to keep from dying is to divert blood from the arms and legs to keep it close to the heart and your core. This rerouting is exactly why your hands and feet get cold first. Your body then shivers in order to generate heat. But don't be fooled: That shivering, which can be comedic, is a sign that all is not well. Before long, your muscles fatigue, and the shivering ceases. You haven't warmed up when your body stops shivering. Instead, you've merely gotten tired. You may even feel so warm that you strip off a layer or two of winter clothing. Many hypothermia victims, because of what is called "paradoxical undressing," are actually found partially clothed or even naked. Here's what you can do to help your body fight the cold.

WEAR A HAT You know how your grandma told you that you lose most of your body heat out of your head? Well, the truth is you lose heat from whatever's uncovered. Which is often your head. So those beanies (A) are more than fashion. At least in winter, they can be lifesavers.

KEEP YOUR COAT ON Wear an appropriate winter coat (B) to keep you both warm and dry during cold weather. You want something that is windproof as well as wicking, meaning that it pulls moisture away from your body.

CHANGE CLOTHES If you're working outside, take time every hour or so to go back in and get dry clothes on (C). Wet fabrics leach body heat.

WATCH THE SHIVERING If you're feeling freezing cold outside and then start to feel warmer, but the ambient temperature has remained steady, it's time to go inside and warm up. Don't delay (D).

034 COME IN FROM THE COLD SAFELY

When you've been out shoveling your way out from under that latest blizzard, a cup of hot chocolate and a roaring fire in the fireplace probably sound like the best things in the world. But it helps to take a few simple precautions to make sure you warm up properly.

Chances are, your extremities like fingers and toes have grown incredibly cold. The best way to warm them up is by surprising your partner with frozen hands on their warm skin. All joking aside, though, don't go run your digits under hot water right away. Instead, start with cold water, which still will be warmer than your cold skin. Gradually warm up the water until you're feeling normal again.

On a much larger scale, climbing into a steaming hot shower or sauna can cause dizziness and even unconsciousness in rare cases. So if you have been out and are cold, wet, and in need of a warm-up, strip out of your wet clothes first, and follow the same approach as you did to warm up your hands. Start with colder water first, and gradually increase the heat as your body warms up.

035 SAVE YOUR ROOFTOP

Sure, a winter wonderland is delightful as long you get to stay inside drinking hot toddies and playing games. But while you're safe, sound, and cozy inside, the weather outside really can be frightful, with heavy snows accumulating at several inches per hour. Depending on the type, snow can weigh as little as 7 pounds per cubic foot (think of that as pretty, light, fluffy snow) to 20 pounds per cubic foot in the case of drifting, compacted snow. That weight can be one of the biggest factors causing storm damage. Snow piling up on your roof can trigger a collapse, which would obviously be bad news during a blizzard. The same holds true for outbuildings and any trees or aboveground structures. Given this, you should do your best to keep ahead of the snowfall by removing it frequently.

Consider investing in a snow rake, a handy device that lets you remove roof snow from the ground. If not, at least avoid standing under the eaves hoping to knock the snow off the overhang. If you decide to climb on the roof, shovel from the peak of the roof down to the edges, so that you always have firm footing above the snow, and you won't fall should the pack break free and slide off the edge. Also, shovel a path to any vital areas outside so you can get there easily. And keep your trees trimmed back away from your house well before a storm comes.

036 SHOVEL SNOW SAFELY

Every year you hear of folks who have heart attacks while shoveling snow, but even young, healthy folks can injure themselves if they're not careful. Here are a few tips to make sure that no one has to shovel you out when you attempt this chore.

USE THE RIGHT SHOVEL The best shovel has a curved handle that allows you to hold it comfortably when your knees are bent and your back is very slightly flexed (A). A plastic shovel blade will be lighter than a metal one, thus putting less stress on your back. Grip the handle and shaft of the shovel with your hands at least 12 inches apart.

WARM UP This is serious exercise (you can burn about 500 calories an hour shoveling, and work a lot of muscles), so take it seriously. Stretch a little before you shovel (B), and don't shovel when your muscles are already cold.

PUSH IT You want to push the snow along (C) rather than lifting it. If you do have to lift it, lift just as you would any heavy object . . . squat and lift with your legs, not your back. A full shovel-load of wet snow can weigh as much as 25 pounds!

037 DRIVE RIGHT IN WINTER

One of the benefits of winter storms is that they're largely predictable. Government agencies, meteorologists, and news outlets do a good job of getting the word out about impending storms. Yet each year, hundreds of motorists find themselves stranded and ill-prepared to face the storms. Why? A lot of times, that prediction of snow at 4 o'clock in the afternoon leads people and businesses to push to get the most out of their days, leaving them in harm's way when the storms hit. You don't need to hole up in fear. Just be prepared.

- ☐ Make sure someone knows where you are going at all times.

- ☐ Equip a winter survival kit in your car, even if you think it's overkill. Include high-energy foods like raisins, and small packs of food that can be eaten hot or cold. Also, toilet paper.

- ☐ Keep your survival kit inside the car in case your trunk is frozen shut.

- ☐ Keep your car's gas tank at least half full.

- ☐ If you find yourself stuck, tie a fluorescent tie (from your survival kit) to the antenna.

- ☐ Don't drain your battery using emergency flashers. Turn them on only if you hear approaching vehicles. Instead, turn your dome light on. A dim light can be seen from a great distance in the dark of night.

- ☐ A lit candle can warm the interior of a snowed-in car by several degrees, and can keep you alive if need be. Keep thermal hand warmers as well.

- ☐ Keep a small hand shovel handy to help dig yourself out of drifting snow.

- ☐ Keep snow off your car so you are visible to rescue workers, and make sure your exhaust pipe is unblocked.

- ☐ Stay calm. Stick with your car unless you can see shelter and can get to it quickly.

- ☐ Keep your car warm by starting the engine and turning the heater on at regular intervals (no more than 10 minutes per hour). Keep a window cracked to make sure you have fresh air.

- ☐ Always know exactly where you are when driving, and use a cell phone to call 911 if you find yourself stranded. Be as thorough and accurate as you can.

038 SURVIVE IN A SNOWBOUND CAR

If you're stuck in a blizzard, a vehicle can protect you from wind and snow, and its visibility ups the odds that a search crew will find you. But in bitter cold, your car can feel like a freezer, because metal and glass offer little insulation.

PILE IT ON If you are out driving in snowy conditions, keep a shovel in the trunk. A foot of snow piled on the car's roof and trunk will turn it into a cozy-ish metal-lined snow cave.

HEAT THINGS UP Wear all the clothing you have in the car and run the heater in short bursts. Just don't use it constantly (you'll run out of gas), and clear snow from the exhaust pipe periodically to prevent carbon monoxide poisoning. Don't run the engine more than 10 minutes per hour. Keep candles in the car.

STAY VISIBLE Keep snow off the car's hood so searchers can spot the color contrast from the air. Tying a colored strip of cloth to your vehicle's antenna can also help.

KEEP MOVING Exercise every so often inside the car to keep your circulation going. This will also keep you from falling asleep—which can be deadly if it's cold enough.

EXTREME WEATHER AROUND THE WORLD:
SIBERIA

Outside of the poles, the only place on Earth that's instantly synonymous with "bitter cold" is Siberia. The landlocked region is far away from the moderating effects of warmer water, so the land undergoes severe radiational cooling at night. If that isn't bad enough, Siberia is frequently under the influence of the polar vortex, allowing cold air to pool across the region. As snow falls and colder air takes hold, Siberia becomes the natural equivalent of an air conditioner.

Siberia also is a land of extremes. The city of Verkhoyansk is notorious for the greatest swing between cold winter temperatures and warm summer temperatures. The city's climate is so wacky that there's a 189°F difference between the city's record high (99°F) and its record low (-93.6°F).

039

BEWARE OF FREEZING RAIN

Every once in a while during a winter storm, you might look out the window and see that it's raining even though temperatures are far below freezing. This phenomenon, known as freezing rain, is the most dangerous of all the precipitation types.

Cold air is notoriously stubborn; it's very dense, so it likes to hug the ground for long periods of time. In some cases, a layer of warmer air will approach this cold, dense air and not be able to erode it (remember: it's very stubborn), so the warm air will ride up and over the cooler air. This creates an atmospheric setup like a sandwich— you have the subfreezing layers of air acting as the bread, with a pocket of above-freezing air in between like a dangerous slice of meat.

If the precipitation falls into this kind of temperature profile, it starts out as snow in the clouds. Once the snowflakes hit the warmer air, they then melt into liquid rain. All these liquid raindrops then fall through the subfreezing air near the surface, but they can't freeze, since they are completely melted. The raindrops drop to below freezing, becoming supercooled. Once these supercooled droplets reach the ground, they freeze on contact with any exposed surfaces, leaving an accretion of ice.

Any glaze of ice is dangerous for pedestrians and drivers, but once ice reaches a thickness of one-quarter of an inch, it starts to pose a hazard to trees and power lines. This ice accretion can grow several inches thick in the worst ice storms. Ice is extremely heavy, so widespread power outages are common after freezing rain; a thick crust of ice can cause even the loftiest and largest transmission towers to crumple to the ground like paper.

041 IMPROVISE SNOWSHOES

Got some paracord? Got a knife? Then you have all that you need to lash together a set of emergency snowshoes. If you don't have these crucial items go back, read the survival kit item again, and check us when you're ready!

STEP 1 Cut a couple of nice, flexible branches, each at least 3 feet in length. Then, cut a couple of small pieces about 6 inches each, and a couple of about 10 inches.

STEP 2 Bend each long branch into a teardrop shape, and lash it together at the narrow end.

STEP 3 Lace paracord in a zigzag pattern the entire length of each shoe.

STEP 4 Test the snowshoe's size.

STEP 5 Add some bracing crosspieces where your toe and heel will fall.

STEP 6 Lash your boots to the snowshoes.

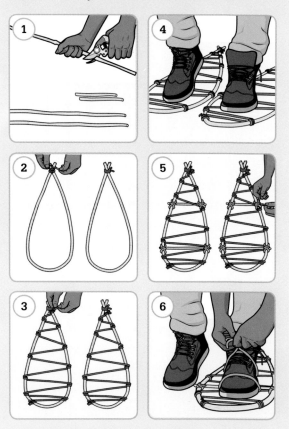

040 BUILD A FIRE ON SNOW

If you're out in the wilderness unexpectedly (or if the snow was unexpected), you might not be prepared to build a fire in snowy conditions. Here's how.

STEP 1 Use rocks or branches to elevate the fire's base above snow-covered or damp ground. Build your fire on a two-layer fire platform of green, wrist-thick (or larger) branches to raft your blaze above deep snow cover. Lay down a row of 3-foot-long branches and then another perpendicular row on top. Stay away from overhanging boughs; rising heat will melt snow trapped in foliage.

STEP 2 Lay out the fuel and don't scrimp on this step. Collect and organize plenty of dry tinder and kindling and get twice as many large branches as you think you'll need. Super-dry tinder is critical; birch bark, pine needles, wood shavings, pitch splinters, cattail fluff, and the dead, dry twigs from the sheltered lower branches of conifers are standards. Place tinder between your hands and rub vigorously to shred the material. You will need a nest as least as large as a Ping-Pong ball. Pouring rain and snow? Think creatively: dollar bills, pocket lint, fuzzy wool, and a snipped piece of shirt fabric will work.

STEP 3 Plan the fire so it dries out wet wood as it burns. Place a large branch or dry rock across the back of the fire and arrange wet wood across the fire a few inches above the flame. Don't crisscross; laying the wood parallel will aid the drying process.

042 COLD-PROOF A SHOTGUN

Some of the best duck hunting takes place in some of the worst conditions for your shotgun: bitter, bone-numbing, oil-thickening cold. Semiautomatic shotguns in particular are at risk for freezing up in temperatures that drop into the teens or even lower. The first aid that some hunters turn to—additional lubrication of the action—is actually the worst possible solution you could use. Lubricants can thicken, especially when mixed with powder residue and grime, and gum up the action. Here's what to do to make sure your scattergun performs in the next "polar vortex."

STRIP THE OIL Disassemble the barrel, receiver, and action. Spray metal parts with Break-Free CLP. Wipe all excess oil away, and wait a few minutes. Now give the parts another good wipe. Use cotton swabs to soak up any excess pooling in nooks and crannies. You want to remove any and all oil. In the field, even a squirt of lighter fluid can serve as an emergency de-gunker.

DUST BATH Use powdered graphite to dust primary action parts such as bolt rails and ejection latches.

OUTSIDE STORAGE Many problems occur when a warm gun is brought into cold, outside air. Moisture condenses on metal gun parts, then freezes in the field. The night before a hunt, store your gun safely outside.

043 BUILD A WILDERNESS SURVIVAL KIT

The average camper, hunter, or outdoors enthusiast may not have much need of a serious winter survival kit, but if you're heading out for a fun day in the woods, you should be prepared. An unexpected snowstorm can turn a day trip into a survival scenario, and you should always be prepared, just in case. Here are the basics to meet your essential needs.

SHELTER A Space blanket, extra clothing, a bivy sack, and even large garbage bags can all provide much needed protection from the elements. Remember that exposure is a top threat in cold environments, so shelter is always your top priority.

FIRE Carry fire gear like lighters, waterproof matches and other fire makers scattered throughout your equipment—you should have at least three options in case something gets lost or fails. You should also include some fire starting fuel, like cotton balls with Vaseline, candle nubs, or commercial fire starter products.

WATER A metal cup, bowl ,or pot to boil water can help provide you a safe and unlimited water supply. Purification tablets and a container for water should also be on your list, as these make water treatment much easier than boiling.

LIGHT Bring several light sources like a flashlight and head lamp which are both rugged and waterproof. Don't forget to pack some extra batteries.

SAFETY This group is a diverse and based on the hazards you'll face. Sun screen and goggles can protect your skin and vision. Bear spray can fend off marauding animals. Work gloves will save your hands from all the wear and tear of performing survival skills. Carry the gear to protect yourself from likely hazards. To signal, carry a whistle. Also bring a signal mirror, which carries much further than the whistle. Don't forget your cell phone, either.

TOOLS Carry a quality knife for dozens of obvious reasons. Cordage is another vital multi-use tool to carry. Duct tape should be part of every survival kit, and it's even flammable.

NAVIGATION Bring a compass and local map, or a GPS with extra batteries, so that you can navigate.

FIRST AID You'll also need first aid equipment to treat wounds and illness, and prevent infection.

FOOD Since the cold can suck the calories out of you in a hurry, bring an emergency food supply along for the energy to keep going. You'll have more strength and you'll also sleep warmer at night with a little food in your belly.

044 DRIVE ON BLACK ICE

One of the most deadly results of freezing rain is the formation of black ice on the roadways. Of course it isn't actually black; this form of ice is so named because it creates a clear glaze on the pavement, making it very difficult to spot. Your best strategy for driving on black ice is not to, but sometimes you'll hit it unexpectedly. Be ready—never use cruise control on wet or icy roads.

STAY CALM When you feel your car losing traction, the worst thing you can do is panic and overreact, which could send your car into a potentially fatal spin.

DO LITTLE The best course is usually to keep the steering wheel straight, keep your foot off the brakes, and hope that your car glides forward over the ice without incident, as black ice patches rarely extend for more than 20 feet.

CORRECT CAREFULLY If you feel your back end starting to slide, turn the steering wheel as gently as you can into the direction of the skid. Trying to turn it the opposite direction will likely lead to a spin-out.

EASE OFF You never want to brake, but you can slow down by taking your foot off of the accelerator. If you can, shift into low gear.

045 SLIP-PROOF YOUR BOOTS

A trip to an outdoor store will show you a wide range of fancy and expensive footwear designed to protect you from a painful and embarrassing fall on your rear in slippery winter conditions. But you don't have to spend big bucks to be slip free.

Visit your local golf shop and purchase some screw in cleats for your favorite winter shoes or boots. They work as well as studded tires on your vehicle in similarly slippery conditions. You may have to drill small holes in your soles to get them started, but what you'll save in dignity is worth the effort.

WEATHER WORLD RECORDS
HIGHEST AIR PRESSURE

One of the main complaints that drives our older relatives down south for the winter is that the cold air makes their joints hurt. There is some truth to that—higher pressure accompanies cold air, which can also increase the pressure on the fluid inside your joints. Knees were especially achy in Tosontsengel, Mongolia, on December 30, 2004, when the village set the world record for the highest air pressure ever recorded at 1089.1 millibars.

046 WATCH OUT WHEN THE SNOW MELTS

One of the scariest prospects after a season of heavy snow is the possible risk of temperatures rising just high enough to allow precipitation to fall as a cold rain instead of snow or even ice. A dense snowpack on the ground can be a recipe for disaster if a heavy rain threatens, as the rain will have few places to go unless all natural and man-made drainage systems are completely clear of snow and debris.

Once the heavy rain begins to fall onto a thick snowpack, it puddles anywhere it can, including against the walls of buildings and in parking lots. This scenario is particularly dangerous, because it can cause roof collapses. Every winter, countless buildings from homes to big-box stores suffer roof damage from the weight of rain falling on top of accumulated snow.

The best way to prevent this kind of flooding and damage from winter rains is to clear any snow away from sewers and drainage pipes immediately after a storm. Try (safely, of course!) to remove any excess snow from your roof and gutters before it begins to melt, freeze, or rain, so that you don't have to worry about your roof sustaining any leaks or structural damage from the weight of the slush.

047 FEEL THE FREEZE

Fog is a spooky and beautiful sight that is common during the late fall and early winter. Fog is little more than a cloud that forms at the surface, a result of water vapor condensing when the air reaches its saturation point. In most cases, the greatest danger that accompanies fog is reduced visibility, which can make travel by boat, plane, or car a dangerous proposition at times, especially when the fog is so thick you can't see more than a few feet in front of you.

FREEZING FOG

Fog during the winter months carries an added danger: It can freeze. Freezing fog is a relatively rare but exceedingly dangerous form of fog that develops when air temperatures are well below freezing. Freezing fog looks and feels just like regular fog, but it can deposit ice crystals on any exposed surfaces outdoors, leaving a glaze of ice on roads and sidewalks.

RIME ICE

When air temperatures are solidly below freezing and the freezing fog is persistent, then a gorgeous phenomenon called rime ice can develop. Rime ice forms when the deposition of ice crystals begins to accumulate beyond a simple glaze, leaving thick, intricate ice formations on trees, railings, cars, and even windows. The spectacular result can look like a beautiful coating of snow.

048 SPOT NATURE'S OWN SNOWBALLS

One of the most confusing types of precipitation that can occur is graupel. Is it snow or sleet? Well, graupel is like snow's weird cousin that shows up at odd times and makes a mess of things. On rare occasions, supercooled water vapor can deposit ice on falling snowflakes, much in the same way that freezing fog can create rime ice on trees and lampposts.

By the time these rimed-up snowflakes reach the ground, they look like tiny snowballs, closely resembling the appearance and consistency of Dippin' Dots (if you're familiar with the tasty treat). Graupel can land on surfaces with a "tink" that sounds like sleet, but it accumulates and acts like snow in every other way. You can pick up a handful of graupel without damaging it, but if you try to manhandle a piece of graupel, it will crumble like a fragile snowflake. There, now you can impress your friends with your knowledge of weird weather stuff.

049 BEAT ICE ON THE CHEAP

Ice is no fun to drive on. You know that. But did you know that you can deal with it without spending much? Here are some frugal tips to keep you from spinning your wheels—literally and figuratively.

LITTER A LITTLE Buy two bags of inexpensive kitty litter and throw them in your trunk before the first signs of winter. If you do get in a pickle and can't get traction, simply break open a bag and spread it in front of your tires. Once you get rolling, your problems will be solved.

HIT THE MAT The next time you're stuck on ice or crusty snow and rocking your vehicle won't bounce you out of the rut, try taking your vehicle's floor mats out and pushing them as far under the front edge of your tires as possible. Your tires will grip the mats and allow you to drive forward.

050 MEET SLEET

The sound of sleet can be comforting or grating, depending on your mood. If you open up your door and hear a noise that sounds like endless grains of rice dropping into a giant metal bowl, chances are you're experiencing sleet. Sleet, also called ice pellets, is an paradoxical type of precipitation that acts like snow, but can cause as much danger and annoyance as ice.

Sleet forms in a very similar manner to freezing rain. Its formation involves a shallow layer of warmth sandwiched in between layers of subfreezing air in the clouds and at the surface. The difference between sleet and freezing rain lies in the melting of the snowflake. The shallow layer of warm air only lets the snowflake partially melt, leaving some ice crystals mixed in with the raindrop.

WEATHER WORLD RECORDS
APOCALYPTIC ICE

One of the worst ice storms in recent recorded history occurred across parts of New England and eastern Canada in early January 1998. The unprecedented storm left behind more than 5 inches of solid ice on trees, power lines, and any other exposed surfaces. The storm destroyed vast swaths of the power grid, paralyzing cities like Ottawa and Montreal, and disrupting the lives of millions of people for weeks and months after the storm.

051 WINTERIZE YOUR RIDE

When most of us hear a forecast that includes severe winter weather, we typically either plan on taking a day off from work or just figure that the commute will be a little slower than usual. Few of us anticipate things going seriously wrong and getting stuck in a car somewhere. But it can happen, and it only takes a small bit of time and effort to prep your car for a possible winter emergency. Here's what you should be sure you have onboard when the weather gets frosty.

CELL PHONE CHARGER Even in the best of weather, we've all ended up with a dead phone battery. Don't let it happen when you're stuck and in danger.

WATER Safe drinking water is a critical item, even in winter. You don't have to be hot to dehydrate. Keep a gallon jug in your trunk per person in the car.

FLASHLIGHTS Keep several lights and some spare batteries. A headband light can be especially useful, keeping your hands free while you work on a broken down car or rummage through the trunk in the dark.

FLARES These can be used to signal roadside distress, but also to start a survival fire if need be.

JUMPER CABLES Car batteries will be especially vulnerable in winter months.

TOW STRAP A nylon tow strap can help you to get your vehicle out of a ditch or snowbank.

FIRST AID KIT Sometimes the vehicle will need repair, and sometimes it's a person who needs mending.

FULL-SIZED SPARE, TIRE IRON, AND JACK Check your tires often in winter. If roads are snowy and icy, you can have a flat and not even know it.

BLANKETS AND/OR SLEEPING BAGS If you've got a four-person car, carry four sleeping bags.

FOOD You probably don't need to stock up on heavy dinner items, but high-energy treats are great.

WINTER EXTRAS There are any number of extra items to help keep you comfortable if you're stranded in a car: a signal flag, tea candles, chemical hand warmers, and the like. When in doubt, include it.

052 IGNORE THE POLAR VORTEX PANIC

Sometimes part of survival is just knowing what not to worry about. The polar vortex is a perfect example. This phenomenon has been so overhyped by the media that if you didn't know any better, you would think the common weather feature, which happens a few times a year, was some sort of mythical creature that swoops down from the Arctic to kill people and steal all of our milk and bread. The old saying, "If it bleeds, it leads," is still valid, but news organizations today have found that scaring people is a much better hook than showing them gory scenes.

The first description of the polar vortex appeared back in the Fall 1853 edition of *Littell's Living Age*. In old-fashioned language, the text describes how air is heated by the sun at the Equator, then gracefully flows northward until it "is whirled about the [North] pole in a continued circular gale," which the author called a "polar vortex."

While the media didn't create the term—it predates CNN by about 127 years, after all—they did hype it into a doomsday scenario, as if the recent polar vortex were the first of its kind. Lobes and pieces of the polar vortex break off and swing south on a regular basis—people have just finally learned the name for it.

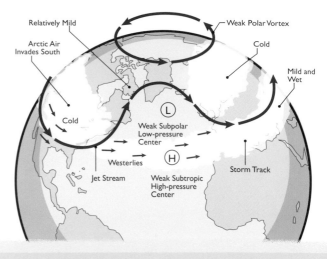

053 MAKE PEACE WITH THE POLAR VORTEX

As discussed above, the very name "polar vortex" sounds ominous, and since 2014, we've had to endure endless media-driven panic over this common feature. Trust me—it's not as scary as the media tries to make it sound.

The polar vortex is an ever-present air circulation in the upper levels of the atmosphere that wraps around the Arctic like a moat, keeping the cold air locked in place over the far northern latitudes where it belongs. The polar vortex circulation looks like a smooth belt, separating bitterly cold air (sometimes colder than -40°F at the surface) from slightly warmer (warmer is relative here) air to its south.

Every once in a while, a large ridge of high pressure builds across western North America, forcing the polar vortex circulation over the Arctic to break down. When the vortex breaks down, two things can happen. In the first scenario, the polar vortex circulation becomes elongated, digging a sharp trough down into southern Canada and the United States. In the second scenario, a piece of the circulation actually breaks off into its own upper-level low-pressure system, which could then circulate down over the same regions and bring its own frosty weather.

Not every tango with bitterly cold Arctic air is a result of the polar vortex, but any trough or cut-off low associated with the polar vortex that dips down over the lower latitudes during the colder months can result in temperatures well below average, with readings often dipping below zero for the duration of the event. Will you get cold? Sure. Will you die some new and peculiar death? Nope.

EXTREME WEATHER HISTORY:
THE POLAR VORTEX, JANUARY 2014

The cold snap heard 'round the world—the one that thrust the polar vortex into everyday conversation—occurred at the beginning of January 2014. On January 4, the main circulation of the polar vortex got wedged in between a strong ridge over the West Coast and a strong high over Canada's Hudson Bay. With nowhere else to go, it raced south toward the Upper Midwest. The center of the circulation resided over central Wisconsin on the morning of January 6, bringing record-breaking cold weather to much of the region.

Low temperatures on January 6, 2014, were staggering: Chicago saw a low of -16°F, Minneapolis dipped to -23°F at its coldest, while International Falls, Minnesota, recorded a low of -30°F. The following morning, Detroit dropped to -14°F, Indianapolis to -15°F, and New York City down to a balmy 4°F.

The cold snap of January 2014 was brutal, sure, but it pales in comparison to temperatures we've seen in the past.

One of the worst cold snaps in American history occurred on January 20–21, 1985, as a result of the polar vortex's main circulation moving over the northern United States. The feature tormented the Upper Midwest with low temperatures close to -35°F in spots on January 20. The following day, the blast dove south, bringing subfreezing air as far south as Miami, Florida, shattering all-time record lows for many southern cities. National Airport in Washington, D.C., bottomed out at -4°F that morning, forcing President Ronald Reagan to take his second oath of office inside the Capitol Building instead of on its west steps, as is customary for presidential inaugurations.

ICY SIDEWALKS ARE TOO DANGEROUS

Walking on an icy sidewalk is a dangerous adventure that can lead to broken bones or worse. But contrary to popular belief, it's not completely impossible to walk on ice. Instead of walking normally (heel-toe, heel-toe), walk slowly and with a flat foot to distribute your weight over a wider surface area. This technique makes it possible to more safely walk on ice without risking injury or an embarrassing slip-and-fall video surfacing online.

054 CHOOSE WOOD WISELY

Most of us are perfectly fine without hot food for a day or two while we wait for the power to come back on. But in extreme weather emergencies, time is a luxury we may not have. When the temps drop low enough to be dangerous, blankets and quilts may not be enough to do the trick. If you resort to burning wood for either cooking or heat, it's important to know what you're burning. Pressure-treated wood, like what's found in landscaping timbers and railroad ties, contains chemicals that can fill a house with toxic smoke. The same thing goes for many painted woods, so don't just go randomly tearing apart your furniture to burn in an emergency. Your best bet is to have some dry, seasoned wood available. Even if you don't have your own chimney and a fireplace inside, it's a good idea to have something burnable handy during the winter months. If that seems a little too extreme, at least have a plan for what you can and can't burn in an emergency.

EXTREME WEATHER AROUND THE WORLD: HIMALAYAS

The Himalayas' location and proximity to the moisture-rich Indian Ocean allows for explosive snowstorms to envelop the range, leaving the highest elevations covered in snow and ice the whole year. Hundreds of people have died on Mount Everest alone, many of whom were caught in blizzard conditions or avalanches while ascending or descending the peak.

Some of the worst snowstorms in the world occur in the Himalayas, including one in October 2014. The remnants of tropical cyclone Hudhud crossed India and ran up against the southern slopes of the Himalayas; the combined effects of tropical moisture, orographic lift (rising air that's produced by wind flowing up the side of a mountain), and frigid temperatures resulted in more than 6 feet of snow falling in some locations.

055 KNOW THE LOWS

Like most of us, nature just wants some peace and quiet. Unfortunately, the only way it can achieve peace is to achieve balance, and it is for this very Zen-like reason that weather happens. Nature abhors a vacuum, so air will rush to fill any area of lower pressure in the atmosphere. The resulting winds can produce intense lifting motions, resulting in everything from simple clouds to raging thunderstorms.

Why does this matter to you as you plan your day? The vast majority of weather around the world is often caused by some form of low pressure. Elongated, open areas of lower pressure—called troughs—are the most common features we deal with. Troughs can exist from the ground to the jet stream, but the most important troughs are in the upper levels of the atmosphere. Large-scale lift is common downwind of an upper-level trough, so if you see one on a map to your west, active weather is a good bet.

We're most familiar with those big, closed lows that can stretch across entire countries. Since winds circulate counterclockwise around the lows in the Northern Hemisphere, these systems often drag warm air from the south and cold air from the north, creating warm and cold fronts, respectively. These frontal systems can produce enormous amounts of lift, allowing widespread (and sometimes heavy) precipitation to form.

056 BEWARE THE WRATH OF THE JET STREAM

It is nearly impossible to listen to a weather forecast without hearing about the jet stream. It doesn't seem like a fast-moving river of air more than 30,000 feet above the ground would have much of an effect on us mere surface dwellers, but it is the driving force behind some of the most powerful storms nature can throw at us.

For the most part, the jet stream is caused by a difference in temperatures between the north and the south. Pockets of extremely strong winds embedded in the jet stream—sometimes screaming along at more than 200 MPH—are known as jet streaks, and these jet streaks are crucial in the development of strong lows, especially during the winter.

If you're unfortunate enough to get caught near the wrong end of a jet streak, your weather could go downhill in a hurry. These jet streaks are roaring so quickly that they can suck air out of the surrounding atmosphere in a process called divergence. Since nature strives for balance, air rushes up toward the jet stream from the ground in order to fill the void. The sudden loss of air from the surface creates an area of low pressure.

Areas of divergence around the jet stream are the fuel that can power a winter storm for days at a time, dumping feet of wind-driven snow on the unlucky residents caught in the path of their fury.

Jet Stream

057

IDENTIFY THE WORST WEATHER

During every wintry nor'easter, there's always that one small town that gets slammed with more snow than anyone else. All that it takes is one heavy band of snow to beef up accumulations and turn a run-of-the-mill storm into a historic, memorable fiasco. The heaviest band of snow in a nor'easter is the result of a feature called the deformation zone, and unlucky towns caught underneath it can see several feet of snow by the time the storm leaves the area.

A deformation zone is a part of a low-pressure system where warm and cold air collide in the middle to upper levels of the atmosphere. When these air masses collide with each other, the zone stretches out (or deforms), creating enhanced lift that results in a band of extremely heavy snow. These features create the classic "comma head" that we see on satellite images of intense winter storms. Deformation zones aren't exclusive to nor'easters, but they're highly disruptive in these storms because they tend to set up over tens of millions of people.

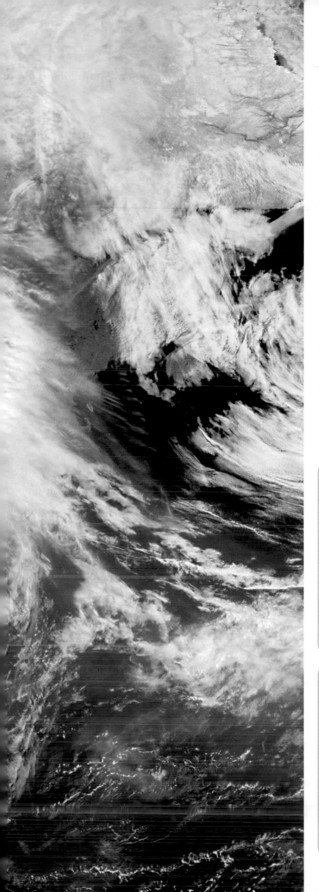

058 KEEP TABS ON THE MILLERS

As if it weren't hard enough to keep track of every different kind of weather system that tries to kill us, there are two different kinds of nor'easters that you have to look out for. The first can provide New England and Atlantic Canada with a pretty solid thumping, while the second can affect tens of millions of people from Florida to the Arctic Circle.

The two types of nor'easters are called Miller Type A and Type B, named in honor of J.E. Miller, the meteorologist who first described them in the mid twentieth century.

Let's start with the weaker, Miller Type B storms. These nor'easters form from weak lows called Alberta Clippers, which scoot southeast out of central Canada toward the Mid-Atlantic and the Carolinas. If there's enough lift from the jet stream, the lows can rapidly strengthen and start moving up the coast toward New England. Type B nor'easters aren't prolific, but they can dump snow on New York, Boston, and Atlantic Canada.

Miller Type A storms are the ones winter haters should fear. Type A storms form near the Gulf of Mexico, so they have plenty of time, space, and moisture to organize into monsters that rake the entire Atlantic seaboard. These systems can produce tornadoes in the southeast, feet of snow along Interstate 95, and flooding in coastal towns, with a storm surge worse than some hurricanes. The Storm of the Century in March 1993 was a classic Miller Type A nor'easter.

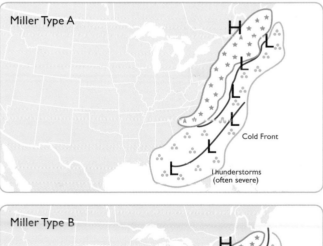

Miller Type A

Cold Front

Thunderstorms (often severe)

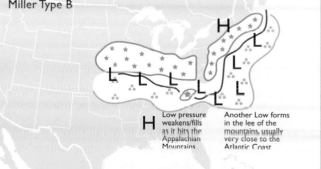

Miller Type B

Low pressure weakens/fills as it hits the Appalachian Mountains

Another Low forms in the lee of the mountains, usually very close to the Atlantic Coast

059 UNDERSTAND NOR'EASTERS

All the major news networks love a good disaster, and especially one that unfolds right outside of their studios. All the immense coverage and legends that surrounding nor'easters is astounding, and just the name can send a shiver down the spine of residents along the east coasts of the United States and Canada. Nor'easters get their name from the stiff, northeasterly winds that batter the coast of New England as they rip through the region.

The power of a nor'easter can rival the strength of a weak hurricane. Kids dream about them for a guaranteed week off from school, while commuters dread them for the gridlock that befalls cities like Washington, D.C., and New York. The legend of the nor'easter focuses mostly on the potential for gobs of snow, but their ugly, less-advertised fury can take the uninitiated by surprise.

060 FOLLOW THE STORM'S TRACK

We love certainty, and we expect no less from our weather forecasts. We want to know exactly when it will snow, how much we'll see, and whether the kids will have to go to school tomorrow (oh please let them have school). Nor'easters are one of those gray areas in meteorology where a small change in the track of the storm can mean big differences in the forecast.

The storm needs to take the right track in order for it to produce blockbuster snows along Interstate 95 from Washington, D.C., to Portland, Maine. If it moves too far offshore, the precipitation will stay along the immediate coast. A track too far inland will make for a sloppy, rainy mess in the megalopolis. The sweet spot is a coordinate over the Atlantic Ocean: 40°N, 70°W. This spot, about 220 miles east-southeast of New York City, is widely regarded as the prime location over which the center of a nor'easter needs to travel in order to produce extreme snowfall over major cities on the U.S. East Coast.

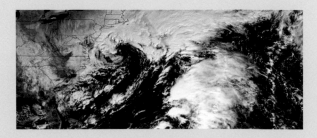

061 PREPARE FOR THE IMPACTS OF A NOR'EASTER

Nor'easters are a snow lover's dream, but they can quickly turn into a nightmare for the amount of damage and trouble they can produce. Here's a look at the different impacts you can expect during one of these severe winter storms.

RISK LEVEL	WHAT TO EXPECT	HOW TO PREPARE	
HEAVY SNOW Very High	Deep accumulations of heavy, wet snow. Impassible roads, tree and roof damage, and unmanageable drifts are possible.	Proactively trim trees and clear snow from your roof to prevent damage. Exercise regularly to reduce risk of injury while shoveling. If you can't handle shoveling, get someone else to do it!	
DAMAGING WINDS High	The strong pressure gradient in nor'easters results in winds that can reach hurricane force.	Secure or bring inside loose items that could blow around and cause damage. Prepare for extended power outages, just as a precaution.	
BEACH EROSION High	Strong winds, waves, and flooding can cause beach erosion. Homes right on the coast can sustain damage (or even get destroyed) by the coast falling into the ocean.	Do your part to keep sand dunes, vegetation, and fences intact so sand builds up and remains on the beaches. If you're right on the coast, prepare to evacuate if things get dicey.	
HEAVY RAIN Medium	When the atmosphere is a little too warm for snow, nor'easters can produce heavy rainfall. A couple of inches of rain are possible.	Rain is harmless unless it falls too heavily for storm drains to handle. Rain falling on snowpack can cause localized flooding and building damage.	
FREEZING RAIN Medium	Ice accretion from freezing rain is possible in that transition zone between regular rain and snow. On rare occasions, significant ice storms can result from nor'easters.	Keep rock salt, sand, and cat litter on hand to help melt ice and provide traction to walk and drive. Also have plenty of food, water, medicine, and cash in case your power goes out.	
STORM SURGE Medium	Strong winds coinciding with high tide can cause a storm surge (push water ashore), as in a minimal hurricane.	Take precautions to prevent flood damage, and evacuate if told to do so by local authorities.	

062 SAFELY SPLIT WOOD

Chopping wood isn't as easy as it looks in the movies. Here's how to get a great bit of exercise while making sure you keep all your fingers and toes.

STEP 1 You'll need a chopping block. This is a thick slab of wood, larger in diameter than the wood you'll be splitting. Saw it parallel on top and bottom, and set it on an even surface.

STEP 2 Place your log on the chopping block.

STEP 3 Chop down with your axe onto the log. Look for a natural split that runs from the outside of the log toward the inside, and aim for that location.

STEP 4 If you're lucky, the log will split on its own. But that's not the goal. The goal is for the axe to stick. With the axe in the log, swing the axe (with the log still intact) around and over your head in a single, circular motion.

STEP 5 As the axe and log move over your head and start downward to the chopping block, rotate the axe so that the dull side strikes the block. The axe will stop. The wood will not. And it will split neatly in two. Repeat as necessary.

A COUPLE OF TIPS Don't chop your logs from a whole tree. Saw them instead. Your axe, contrary to popular belief, doesn't have to be sharp. And if you are splitting logs into kindling and you reach the point that they're falling over on the chopping block, don't hold them with your free hand. It's only a matter of time before you lose a finger. Instead, stabilize them with a piece of wood. For extra safety, use a special wood-splitting wedge and a sledgehammer instead. Less change of cutting yourself, and more efficient. Plus you get to use a sledgehammer! Who doesn't love that?

063 STORE FOOD WITH NO POWER

There's one upside to losing power in the winter: the ease with which you can store perishable food items. Essentially, the world is your freezer.

STEP 1 If there's a decent amount of snow covering the ground, dig yourself a cubby.

STEP 2 Direct contact with snow can damage meat and vegetables, and unpackaged food is also susceptible to hungry scavengers looking for an easy meal. It's best to put all perishable items into individual plastic bags to reduce odors that might attract animals.

STEP 3 Store the packaged items in a wooden box or trunk (even a small side table with a latching door will work) and bury the container in the snow. You may end up losing a piece of furniture, but you'll prolong your food stores—and that trade-off is well worth the sacrifice.

064 FIRE UP A ROCKET STOVE

A few years ago, prior to the prepper movement, most people had never heard of a rocket stove. Long beloved by backpackers and campers, a rocket stove is an insulated cooking stove that creates high heat from small-diameter pieces of wood. All that you need to build your own are a couple of 12-ounce soup cans and a large coffee can or empty, gallon-sized paint can. A bag of kitty litter (all natural and with no preservatives) completes your list.

STEP 1 Cut the top and bottom off one of the soup cans (A). This can will be the feeder tube.

STEP 2 Cut only the top off another one of the soup cans. This will be your burning chamber (B).

STEP 3 Cut the top and bottom off a third soup can. Then use tin snips to cut it open from top to bottom.

STEP 4 Stand the burning chamber can on a surface, then place the feeder tube can near the bottom. Use a marker to trace the circumference of the feeder tube onto the burning chamber.

STEP 5 Use a nail to punch a hole through the burning chamber, and then cut out the circle you've just drawn. Then, place the feeder tube into the base of the burning chamber.

STEP 6 Repeat step 5 on the base of the coffee can (C), then center the burning chamber inside the coffee can. You now should be able to insert the feeder tube through the coffee can and into the burning chamber.

STEP 7 Roll up the third soup can so that you can slide it about half an inch into the top of the burning chamber. Use a piece of wire to tie it in place.

STEP 8 Use your kitty litter (or small rocks, sand, or similar material) to fill up the inside (D) of the large can.

STEP 9 Place a cook surface (you can grab a cast iron burner top off a junked stove) on top of the large can (E).

STEP 10 All you have to do at this point is feed a few small sticks (F) into the feeder tube and light the inside with a long fireplace lighter. Keep feeding the small sticks into the tube to keep the heat high. The efficient stove will heat up in a hurry and allow you to boil water or cook dinner in the event you lose power.

NOTE The first time you fire up the stove, do it outside, as many commercial cans have a toxic coating that will need to be burned off before you use the stove inside on a nonflammable surface.

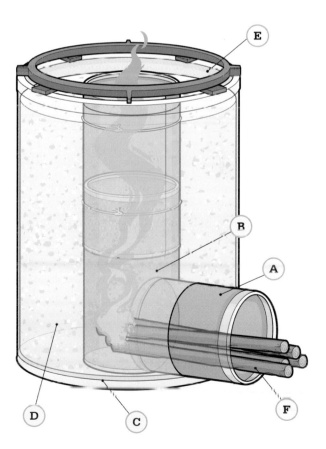

DENNIS DEBUNKS:

YOU WON'T CATCH A COLD FROM THE COLD

One of the stock lines from the Great Book of Mom Sayings is "The cold will make you sick." Fortunately for cold lovers near and far, the cold itself doesn't directly make you sick. But viruses like the flu can linger longer in cold, dry weather, and when you add that to the fact that you're indoors for most of the winter, it's a recipe for a sneezetastrophe of epic proportions.

065 DON'T BURN THE BRISKET

It can be bad enough to be trapped at home by ice, snow, or foul weather. But it would be even worse if your home caught fire while the rescue squad and the fire department were hampered by the conditions. House fires occur often in winter, and the most common time of day for these fires is between 5:00 and 8:00 PM. This may seem odd, until you learn the cause: cooking. According to the U.S. Fire Administration, fires during the winter season cause more than $2 billion worth of damage each year. Most of these events are preventable, so take steps to guard against fire this season.

DO:
Keep anything flammable (like paper towels and any food packaging) at least 1 yard away from your stove or cooktop.

Keep a fire extinguisher handy in the kitchen, and make sure it is rated for grease fires.

Make sure that the oven, burners, and any appliances are turned off when you're done in the kitchen.

DON'T:
Don't leave the kitchen when you're grilling, frying, or broiling food.

Don't throw water, flour, or towels onto a grease fire— These will make it even worse. Instead, use baking soda or an extinguisher. You could also drop a large lid on a flaming pan to suffocate the flames.

Don't try to pick up or move a flaming pan. You're likely to spread the fire and receive painful burns.

066 IDENTIFY A TRUE BLIZZARD

We throw around the term "blizzard" often enough that it seems to have lost any real meaning. We like to think that any heavy snowfall is a blizzard. Six inches of snow? Blizzard. Schools closed? Blizzard. Fifty-car pileup on the highway? Blizzard. Flurries in Florida? Mega blizzard. In the United States, the term has a very specific meaning tied to recorded weather conditions.

A blizzard actually occurs when sustained winds of 35+ MPH create blowing snow that reduces visibility to one-quarter of a mile for three or more consecutive hours. That sounds like an absurd (or at least arbitrary) criterion to meet, but the definition for a blizzard is very close to the definition of a whiteout. Winds that blow snow around hard enough to reduce visibility to almost nothing constitutes a blizzard. Looking out your window during a true blizzard is useless—you can't see more than a few hundred feet down the street, anyway.

067 STAY ORIENTED IN A WHITEOUT

You don't want to get caught outside during a blizzard, and not just because the wind and snow will sting your cheeks and make you feel cold. True blizzard conditions result in whiteouts, a phenomenon where you can't see anything but a wall of white in front of you.

When pilots fly through clouds or fog and can't see beyond their wings, they have instruments to guide them to safety. You do not have that luxury, and it's very easy to become disoriented if you're outside during a blizzard.

Getting caught in a blizzard can be lethal—if you get lost, you could succumb to exposure within a few hours if nobody can rescue you. Do everything in your power to maintain situational awareness. If you are caught in a vehicle during a blizzard, do not try to abandon your car to find shelter. You are safer in your car than you are wandering around a highway where you can't see a thing. If you're at home, as tempting as it may be to go outside, stay indoors unless the place is in flames. If you absolutely must go outside, tie a rope to the doorknob or a railing and hold on to it so you can find your way back to safety. It may look silly, but nobody will be able to see you to judge and laugh.

068 DON'T GET COMPLACENT

Unless you live in the far north, it takes the right set of weather conditions to come together and produce the intense snow and driving winds necessary to create a good ol' blizzard. Between January 2005 and March 2015, the National Weather Service issued 1,260 blizzard warnings for counties across the United States. That seems like quite a few, but more than half of them were issued for the Alaskan tundra—not exactly a populous part of the country.

KNOW YOUR REGION Thanks to their lengthy, brutal winters, you're most likely to experience blizzard conditions if you live in Alaska or visit the Arctic Circle. Farther south, the flat Canadian prairies and American plains are vulnerable to intense winds accompanying heavy snowfall. Residents along the eastern coasts of the United States and Canada (from Washington, D.C., through the Maritimes) also experience blizzards every couple of years, in large part due to powerful nor'easters sweeping through. Blizzards caused by nor'easters carry the greatest impact, since they affect large population centers that are home to tens of millions of people.

STAY AWARE All of that said, blizzards are pretty rare, and just like tornadoes, earthquakes, and hurricanes, the rarity of blizzards can breed complacency. Not every snowstorm is similar, and if you live somewhere like Virginia or Texas and go under a blizzard warning, don't let your guard down because "they never happen around here." If you're unprepared for the effects of the intense winds, driving snow, and bitterly cold temperatures, you could find yourself in a world of trouble.

069
DON'T PILE ON IN A PILE-UP

Having to drive during a snowstorm is unavoidable sometimes, but even a brief period of heavy snow or strong winds that reduces visibility is dangerous on a densely packed highway.

Every few weeks during the winter, we hear stories about dozens of cars involved in a pile-up accident out on a highway somewhere in the northern United States or Canada. All it takes is one person losing control of their vehicle to begin a chain reaction that can mangle dozens of cars and ruin hundreds of lives. Pile-up accidents are most common when visibility is near zero or roads are too icy for tires to maintain traction, leaving one car to slide into the one in front of it.

Avoid driving during a winter storm in the first place, but if you absolutely must, leave plenty of room between you and those around you. If you're involved in a pile-up accident, you're in danger whether you stay in your vehicle or get out. Getting out of your vehicle is the safest option, but only when there's no traffic behind you. Don't stay with your car—get as far off the road as possible so you're not a sitting duck when more cars creep up and crash alongside you. Head for safety, and leave a note on the car with your cell phone number or, if there's no shelter, watch from nearby.

070
THANK THE AIRLINES FOR CANCELING YOUR FLIGHT

Have you ever gotten stuck at the airport due to bad weather? That's a good thing. TIn addition to all of the hazards posed to aircraft by slippery runways and ice buildup on the plane, visibility is a major concern. It's hard enough to drive a car when it's foggy or snowing heavily, let alone blindly guide a multi-ton aircraft going several hundred miles per hour onto a small strip of asphalt surrounded by trees and buildings.

Both airplanes and airports are equipped with special equipment that helps pilots take off and land when visibility is less than optimal. Many modern airports have technology known as the Instrument Landing System that uses radio frequencies to help pilots make a safe landing when it's difficult to see, using their instruments to find the correct heading and proper glide slope. During a heavy snowstorm, however, sometimes these instruments won't be good enough. Even with automated landing systems, pilots will still need to be able to see the airfield at a certain altitude in order to make a safe landing. In addition, ice on the wings can have deadly result. If your flight is canceled due to heavy snow, thank the airlines—it helps when pilots can see where they're flying.

EXTREME WEATHER HISTORY:
BOSTON'S EPIC, RECORD-BREAKING WINTER

The winter of 2014–2015 will go down in the record books as one of the most incredible winters in the history of New England, especially Boston. When all was said and done, Boston's Logan Airport recorded an astounding 110.6 inches of snow between November 2014 and March 2015, almost all of which fell in just one thirty-day window. This was the snowiest winter on record in the city, breaking the previous record of 107.6 inches recorded during the winter of 1995–1996.

Though they saw similar snow totals, the two snowiest winters in Boston's history couldn't be more different. The winter of 1995–1996 was a snow hater's death by a thousand flakes. That season's snow fell over a period of six months, spaced out between smaller storms and larger thumpings. The snowstorms that befell Boston in the winter of 2014–2015, however, came almost all at once. Over the span of just thirty days—January 24, 2015, through February 22, 2015— Boston saw 94.4 inches of snow, with accumulating snow reported on twenty of those thirty days.

071 WATCH OUT FOR TEXAS HOOKERS

A wide range of unusual storm types are associated with low-pressure conditions around the world. But only the U.S. seems to have really awesome names for them. One particularly nasty type of storm is known as a "Panhandle Hook," more commonly called a "Texas Hooker," because that's a much more fun name. A Texas Hooker is a strong low-pressure system that typically develops over the Texas Panhandle and moves (or hooks) northeast toward the Great Lakes over the following couple of days.

Those hookers know how to have a wild time, and they can create some pretty nasty weather as they move through the middle of the United States. Towns that are stuck in the warm section of the storm can see enough instability and wind shear that severe thunderstorms and tornadoes are possible. On the northwestern side of the low, where the air is at or below freezing, a heavy, wind-driven snow can fall, sometimes resulting in accumulations of a foot or more across a wide swath of real estate.

Some towns in the path of these storms can witness the entire spectrum of weather conditions in one day. Theoretically, a town could be destroyed by a tornado in the warm sector of a Texas Hooker, only to get a couple of inches of snow on top of the rubble as the cold air intrudes and rain changes to snow. While they are not always quite that dramatic, one particular Texas Hooker went down in history (and song) when it crossed over Lake Superior on November 10, 1975, sinking the *Edmund Fitzgerald*.

072 HELP SOMEONE WHO'S GONE OVERBOARD

The biggest threat to a man (or woman) overboard is hypothermia, even in warm-ish water—so in winter, it's especially deadly. If you've fallen in, do your best to draw your legs up to your chest and float like a cork rather than a pencil. If you're fortunate enough to have your jeans on when you fall overboard, take them off and knot the legs. You can inflate then them as a makeshift life preserver in a pinch. They just might save your life until help arrives. If you are still onboard a vessel, however, there's a lot you can do if you see someone fall or jump. Given that nearly 100 people have gone overboard from even large cruise liners over the past ten years, if you're at sea, this is one of the most common emergencies you'll encounter.

SHOUT IT OUT Yell "Man overboard!" Even if you're by yourself, yell it out. At least the person in the water will know you're taking action.

KEEP POINTING Anyone who spots someone who is overboard should never take their gaze away from them. People disappear quickly between waves. So point. Keep pointing. And keep shouting until help arrives.

GET A FLOTATION DEVICE Ideally the victim already has one on. If not, throw something to them fast.

TOSS A LIFELINE If you're in a smaller, slower boat (think sailboat), you may be able to avert disaster by immediately throwing a rope to the person in the water.

TURN AROUND Always turn the vessel toward the side from which the victim fell. Never back the boat up to retrieve someone who's fallen in the water, as propellers are deadly.

GET THEM OUT Use a lifeline to haul the victim out of the drink. Never jump in to rescue someone. Leave that maneuver to the Coast Guard rescue swimmers.

WARM THEM UP Start treatment for hypothermia (see item 33) right away while you wait for professional help to arrive.

073 DRINK SNOW

While you probably won't hurt yourself snacking on snow (unless it's contaminated or you've been following the sled dogs a little too closely), it's not a good idea for hydration. In a survival situation, trying to consume snow will make your body burn energy you don't have to spare. To make drinkable water, choose ice over snow if possible it often contains fewer foreign objects that can carry pathogens, and ice will convert to more water than an equal volume of snow. Here are three ways to fill your water bottle from the cold stuff.

DRIP IT To melt snow or ice, snip a pea-size hole in the bottom corner of a T-shirt, pillowcase, or other makeshift fabric bag. Pack the bag with snow and hang it near a fire. Place a container under the hole to catch water melted by radiant heat. To keep the fabric from burning, refill the bag as the snow or ice melts.

COOK IT Melting your ice or snow in a pan risks scorching the pot, which will give the water a burned taste. Avoid this by heating a small amount of "starter water" from your water bottle before adding snow or ice. Place the pot over a low flame or just a few coals and agitate frequently.

HUG IT You may have no other option than to use body heat to melt the snow. If so, put small quantities of snow or ice in a waterproof container and then place the container between layers of clothing next to your body—but not against your skin. A soft plastic bag works better than a hard-shell canteen. Shake the container often to speed up the process.

074 BOAT IN BAD WEATHER

Some lakes dish up big, nasty rollers day after day, but just about any lake can throw up bruising water in the right—or wrong—wind. You should stay off the water when high winds are forecast, but if you misjudge and need to get home safely, here's a strategy that just might save your bacon.

You don't want to pound through endless 4-footers in an 18-foot boat, so tack across the rollers as long as they're not breaking. As the roller approaches, run down the trough parallel to the crest, as far as you can or need to, and slide over the crest into the trough behind it. Then turn the bow straight into the swell and ride up and down the rough spots until you need a break. It's slower going, but it's better than getting beat up for miles.

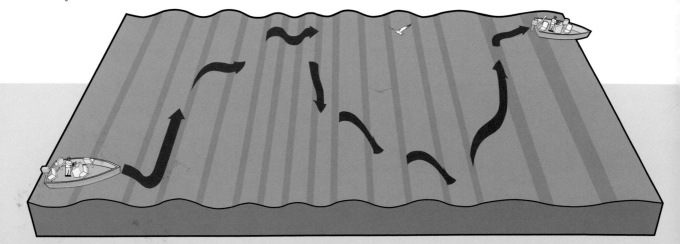

075 CROSS ICE CAREFULLY

Crossing a frozen lake or pond, whether you're ice fishing or you're lost and trying to navigate back to camp, is one of the most dangerous outdoor activities. It's especially perilous towards the end of winter, when the ice pack is deteriorating and thickness alone is not an accurate gauge of safety. Here's how to travel safely.

Slushiness is a sign of a weakening pack; so is finding snow cover or water on top of ice. Depressions in the snow indicate a spring.

Cattails and other vegetation, as well as rocks and logs, conduct heat, weakening the ice.

Stay away from inlet and outlet streams. Under-the-ice current can reduce ice strength by 20 percent or more

Use your walking stick or ice chisel to test ice conditions.

Tow your equipment sled on a long rope. You can push it toward a victim who has fallen through.

A 50-foot cord wrapped around an empty plastic jug makes a handy flotation device. Stand on sturdy ice and toss the jug to the victim.

Beware of black, gray, or milky ice. It lacks the strength of clear blue or green ice.

Eroded shore ice is a sign of a thinning ice pack. Beware.

Thin cracks may let you see whether the ice is thick or not.

Ice sloping from a bank may trap air underneath, reducing its strength.

Pressure ridges are caused by fluctuating temperatures. Avoid them.

Open water is a red flag, pointing to a marginal ice pack nearer the shore.

076
SURVIVE A FALL THROUGH ICE

Forget hypothermia: The first thing to worry about when you've fallen into ice is getting yourself out. Assuming you have your safety spikes (see item 79), here's what to do.

STEP 1 Turn around in the water so you're facing the way you came. That's probably the strongest ice.

STEP 2 Jam the points of the spikes into the ice.

STEP 3 While kicking your feet vigorously, haul yourself out.

STEP 4 As soon as you're on the ice, roll (don't crawl) away from the edge of the hole. Get off the ice, and get warm immediately.

077
PRACTICE SIDEWALK SAFETY

An ice-covered walkway, path, or driveway is the perfect spot for bone-crunching wipeouts and some unnecessary injuries. We've probably all thrown a bit of salt to combat all those treacherous patches of frozen water. But should you use salt on your sidewalks, or are there other options? Sometimes, the decision is made for you and you're stuck just using whatever you have on hand. Table salt, Epsom salt, and rock salt will all melt ice and you may already have them lying around the kitchen or garage. They are, however, harmful to the plants, shrubs, trees, and grass around the walkway. All these salts are also potentially hazardous to pets and livestock who may try to eat them. Before the bad weather arrives, buy a bag of pet-friendly, lawn-friendly product that is made from magnesium chloride, calcium chloride, or related compounds. These are safer and less corrosive forms of salt than sodium chloride (table salt).

And remember that you don't actually have to melt the ice to make your sidewalk passable. Sand, gravel, sawdust, crushed nut shells, non-clumping cat litter, and wood ashes can give your feet some traction on icy surfaces. These traction items are better for the environment, and they are either cheap or free of charge.

DENNIS DEBUNKS:
FROZEN WAVES ARE A THING

Those awesome pictures you see floating around social media every once in a while, excitedly claiming to show "frozen waves" in some super-cold part of the world, are usually mislabeled or just plain fake. Water does not freeze mid-wave in the natural world. These pictures usually show relatively rare blue icebergs (or someone's stellar photo editing skills).

078 DON'T GET CLIPPED

Another type of winter storm that commonly affects southern Canada and the United States is called an "Alberta Clipper." These storms, simply called "clippers" for short, form in south-central Canada in the vicinity of Alberta, but they can also form as far east as southern Manitoba. The storms will then race toward the east or southeast, typically ending on the Atlantic coast in the Mid-Atlantic or the northeastern United States. When an Alberta Clipper approaches your area, you can expect gusty winds, much colder temperatures, and some snow as it passes through the region. Clippers are especially brutal during a cold snap, serving as a reinforcing shot of cold air that can drop temperatures even lower than they were originally.

Clippers typically don't have much moisture to work with, so they generally produce limited amounts of snow. It's enough to make the scenery look pretty and to have to clean off your car, but it's not enough to snarl cities for days on end. However, Alberta Clippers have a nasty habit of catching forecasters and residents off-guard. Every once in a while, these systems can pull more moisture from the south than originally forecast, giving the storm just enough fuel to crank out snow accumulations of 6 or more inches. Under the right atmospheric conditions, clippers can transition into nor'easters once they move off the coast of the Mid-Atlantic or the Northeast.

079 MAKE SAFETY SPIKES

Any chance you might fall through a layer of ice and need to claw your way out? Why not be safe and carry a set of safety spikes with you? They're super easy to make, and can quite literally save your life.

STEP 1 Wrap two Phillips-head screwdrivers in paracord and secure with strong knots, then coat them in foam tape for comfort and floatability.

STEP 2 Wear the spikes underneath your coat with the cord running up your arms and around your shoulders. Let the spikes dangle from your sleeves (or tuck them in your sleeves, if you prefer) when you're on the ice.

WEATHER WORLD RECORDS
SNOWIEST MAJOR CITY IN THE WORLD

Cities like Buffalo, New York, and Moscow, Russia, see quite a bit of snow every year, but they have nothing on the snowiest major city in the world. Sapporo, Japan, serves as home to nearly two million people, and each and every one of them has to deal with nearly 20 feet of snow every year, largely due to the lake-effect (well, sea-effect) snow that pumps ashore from the Sea of Japan.

080 GET READY TO GET SNOWED UNDER

It's hard to imagine 5 feet of snow falling in just a couple of days, but this is what residents of areas that experience the "lake effect" have to contend with. The areas affected by lake-effect snow are called snowbelts, and they include the U.S.'s Great Lakes, the west coast of northern Japan, Russia's Kamchatka Peninsula, and parts of the northern Atlantic Ocean, among others. The warmth of the body of water can create persistent bands of heavy snow that feed over the same areas for hours at a time. The event, called lake-effect snow, is an incredible display of nature's raw power and stamina.

Lake-effect snow develops through a process known as convection—the very same source of lift that produces almost all thunderstorms. Water can retain heat much longer than the air, so lakes take longer to cool down during the fall and winter. As cold, moist air blows over the warmer lakes, the water can heat the air immediately above its surface through conduction, the same way the heat of a pot can bring water to a boil. This warm, less-dense layer of air at the surface rapidly rises through the colder air above, creating the lift necessary for bands of precipitation to develop.

When the air is cold enough and the wind is blowing in the right direction (we'll get into that shortly), these bands of precipitation will come ashore as heavy snow. The impacts of lake-effect snow vary wildly from location to location, with some areas typically seeing a few inches, while others can see several feet.

081 JOIN THE BAND

The two types of lake-effect snow that can affect the Great Lakes are multi-band events and single-band events. The former produce an even snowfall over a widespread area, while the latter can pound just a handful of cities that have so much snow that residents end up needing to climb out of their second-floor windows.

Multi-band lake-effect snow events most commonly occur on the Lakes Superior, Michigan, and Huron, since the orientation of these lakes provides a short fetch when westerly winds take hold. Multi-band events look very much like dozens of tiny fingers tickling the coast when you see them on satellite and radar, and they can produce one to two feet of snow in the most intense situations.

Imagine a box of air over the lake. During one of these events, warm air rises toward the top of the box, hitting the lid and spreading out evenly on both sides. The air will cool and sink on either side, producing a neat column of rising air in the center of the box. Multi-band lake-effect snow works much like this, but the little cells of rising and sinking air are repeated dozens of times. The wind neatly organizes these small convective rolls (as they're called) toward land, where they continue dumping snow until the wind shifts or the convection stops.

082 SIT OUT A SNOWY SINGLE

A little farther to the east, people who live on the eastern shores of Lakes Erie and Ontario are winter-hardy people. They smirk and chortle when you complain about your measly one-foot snowfall in Kentucky. These two lakes are usually aligned parallel to the wind, which allows for some incredible sights in the early winter months.

Unlike multi-band lake-effect snow events, where the little convective cells look like they were printed onto the shoreline with a rubber stamp, single-band events involve almost the entire surface area of the lake. The convective process is the same, but it takes place on a much larger scale. Warm air in the center of the lake rises, spreads out at the top of the atmosphere, and sinks on the body's northern and southern shores. This process allows for a large, thick band of snow to set up and start spraying neighboring towns like a fire hose.

Single bands of lake-effect snow have a bad habit of not moving. If one of these bands stalls out, it's not unheard of for communities caught in the firing line to see 2, 3, or even 4 feet of snow in a single day until the band dissipates or moves elsewhere. Back in 1900, Watertown, New York, sitting on the eastern coast of Lake Ontario, saw nearly 50 inches of snow in one day.

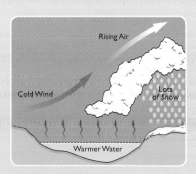

083 BRACE FOR WINTER RAIN

We have the good fortune not to live on a planet like Hoth. In addition to avoiding a brutal intergalactic space battle, even the harshest winter here on Earth will come to an end. The waning days of winter bring melting snow and, inevitably, heavy rains.

The ideal way for a winter's worth of snow and ice to melt is through a gradual warm-up paired with cool nights. This allows the snow and ice to melt nice and slowly, preventing the water from overwhelming drainage systems (both man-made and natural). Some areas are not as fortunate, and they have to deal with beaucoup rainfall toward the end of winter and the beginning of spring.

Heavy rain falling in areas that were hit hard by winter routinely causes issues like ponding on roads and grassy surfaces, and the potential for roof damage. In the worst of cases, the torrent of water with melting snow and ice can cause rivers and streams to overflow, resulting in dangerous flooding. Flooding rain events at the end of winter are most common in mid-latitude regions that experience the four full seasons, including most of the United States, southern Canada, and parts of Europe.

084 USE SANDBAGS

Properly stacked, sandbags are a very effective way to hold back rising waters. Store empty burlap sacks or specially manufactured plastic ones in an accessible place, or get them from your local emergency manager. When the waters start to rise, fill them with sand, ideally. Heavy soil will do in a pinch. Here's how to fill and stack your barrier.

STEP 1 Have one person hold the bag open while a second shovels in sand (or gravel or whatever you have to use).

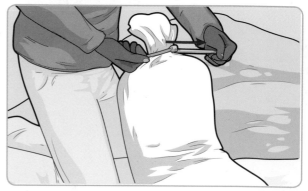

STEP 3 Zip-tie the bag closed. If you don't have zip-ties, you can fold the bags closed as you stack them.

STEP 2 Fill the bag until it's about halfway full.

STEP 4 Layer your bags as shown. If you don't, your barrier will likely leak or topple.

085 FIGURE OUT HOW MANY BAGS YOU NEED

How many sandbags do you need in order to safely protect your home or another area? Doing math while the floodwaters rage sounds crazy, but do you really want to be caught short (or waste time filling more bags than you need, for that matter)? This handy equation will tell you what you need. If you're really smart, you'll calculate how many bags are necessary before the rain falls, so you can swing into action immediately, like the superhero that you are.

Ideally, the base of the sandbag wall should be three times its height. To calculate the number of bags needed per linear foot of wall, the equation is:
(3 x height) + (9 x height x height) divided by 2

So, for a 3-foot-tall wall you need, per foot:
$(3 \times 3) + (9 \times 3 \times 3) / 2 = 45$

If the wall needs to be 5 feet long, that's 5 x 45, for a grand total of 225 bags. Hope you've been hitting the gym: That's a lot of shoveling!

086   PREP YOUR ATTIC

In flood-prone areas, the attic space inside your home can become the most important room in the house. Instead of storing your vital food, supplies, water, and gear at ground level (or worse, in a basement), you can create an ark out of that creepy, dusty attic. Following the ark theme a little further, you should also keep an inflatable raft in the attic to act as a floating storage shelf or means of exit. Have an axe up there, too—or, better yet, a chainsaw. Now you can cut your way out and make an aquatic escape. Remember to cut only a few trusses, to keep the roof from falling in. Wear safety glasses to keep sawdust and shingle grit out of your eyes.

EXTREME WEATHER AROUND THE WORLD:
LONDON

London suffers from one of the most persistent weather stereotypes in the world. Residents and visitors alike regale outsiders with stories of the persistently gray, rainy weather that seems to encompass the major global city on a regular basis. Despite sitting at the same latitude as much of Canada, snow is rare in the southern United Kingdom.

Precipitation tends to stay mostly rain in and around London thanks to a relative lack of cold air flowing south from the Arctic. In southern Canada and the United States, we benefit (or suffer) from very cold air that piles up over the land during the height of winter. The United Kingdom is surrounded by water, which moderates air temperatures during the winter because water can hold heat longer than land.

The effect is exacerbated by a warm current in the Atlantic Ocean known as the Gulf Stream. This current originates in the Caribbean and the Gulf of Mexico, bringing considerably warmer waters all the way to the northern Atlantic near the United Kingdom. The water has a moderating effect on winters in this region, allowing precipitation to fall as rain instead of snow during most storms that sweep through.

087 BEWARE OF DAMAGING WINDS

Damaging winds are a dangerously underestimated force during severe thunderstorms. The U.S. National Weather Service's standards dictate that any thunderstorm that produces winds (sustained or gusts) of at least 58 MPH is strong enough to cause damage to trees, power lines, and buildings, allowing the storm that produced it to be considered "severe."

The most common way for a severe thunderstorm to produce wind damage during the winter months is when the storms organize into a formation called a "squall line." Winter squall lines usually form along the leading edge of a cold front, where atmospheric lift is the strongest and storms are able to focus themselves into a line.

One of the worst widespread wind damage events in the winter months occurred during the Storm of the Century in March 1993. A devastating squall line formed along the historic storm's cold front, causing wind gusts as high as 100 MPH when these thunderstorms swept across Florida and Cuba.

088 MAKE YOUR GARAGE WIND RESISTANT

Battening down the hatches to prepare for a storm? Don't forget the garage. Double-wide garage doors are a weak spot in a windstorm, as high winds can cause these broad, flexible doors to bow inward and even fall off their tracks. And that makes your garage, car, and home vulnerable to greater damage.

You could invest in a wind-resistant door, or reinforce the current door yourself with a kit that will allow you to brace your door and still use it. But if a high-wind advisory has just been issued and you have to act fast, you can board up your garage door with wooden planks, just as you would your home's windows. Add horizontal and vertical bracing onto each panel of the door. If you have an automatic garage-door opener, disable it to avoid accidental damage from someone trying to open the door while it's boarded up.

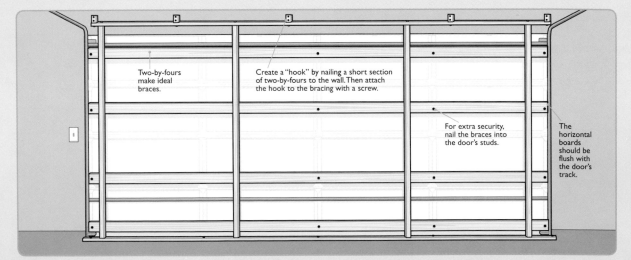

Two-by-fours make ideal braces.

Create a "hook" by nailing a short section of two-by-fours to the wall. Then attach the hook to the bracing with a screw.

For extra security, nail the braces into the door's studs.

The horizontal boards should be flush with the door's track.

089

EXPECT THE UNEXPECTED

Thunderstorms thrive in warm, unstable environments such as those found above tropical and subtropical regions. Some spots, including the Caribbean or the rain forests, see thunderstorms daily, while areas farther north get these rumbling storms so infrequently that one passing through is truly a noted event. Wintertime thunderstorms are most common around the Caribbean and the southern United States, where there's usually enough unstable air seeping in from the south that air can rise and produce heavy rain, thunder, and lightning.

Every once in a while, a strong winter storm will rake across the United States and drag unusually high amounts of instability into the country from the south. These events can result in some explosive severe weather outbreaks. Events such as tornadoes, damaging winds, and large hail can of course be deadly any time of the year, but especially so during the winter when people least expect them to occur. The prevalence of cold, stable air limits how far north these testaments to the power of nature can migrate, but towns as far north as Illinois have to be on alert if they find themselves on the southern end of a powerful winter storm.

Everyone knows that the longest day of the year is the summer solstice, and the shortest is the winter solstice, right? Wrong. The length of the day (sunrise to sunset) is the longest and shortest around the solstices, yes, but the "longest/shortest day of the year" can be every day for a week or longer in places like New York City, London, and Sydney.

090 SURVIVE SEASONAL AFFECTIVE DISORDER

If you live at the North Pole and don't see the sun for months, battling depression will almost be a given (unless you're a vampire, or just really, really goth). But folks around the world fight off some serious blues when the days get shorter. See your doctor if you're really down, and try these pick-me-ups.

LIGHT IT UP Studies show that 15 to 30 minutes in front of a light therapy box can work wonders. For about $100 you can get a small one that you can bask in front of while you have your morning coffee.

GET MOVING Exercise can help regulate your moods. Ideally, you'll be able to walk (or run or sled) outdoors for the benefits of sunshine, but even trotting on a treadmill is helpful.

KEEP A SCHEDULE Having a routine helps keep your brain happy. Unless of course you can toss the schedule entirely and take a tropical vacation. Now that's therapy!

EXTREME WEATHER AROUND THE WORLD:
ARCTIC REGIONS

The poles are the worst places on Earth to have to endure the winter, but there are a handful of residents and scientists who manage to live on or near the North and South Poles during the long, dark winter season. Aside from the cold and snow, the most well-known part of winter in the poles is the longer nights. At the North Pole, the sun rises above the horizon around the spring equinox, appearing to circle the sky for six months until the autumnal equinox, at which point it dips back below the horizon for the long winter. Most towns and villages inside the Arctic and Antarctic Circles don't truly experience total darkness—even on the darkest of days, residents will see a faint glow on the horizon around the middle of the day. It's effectively total night, though, and it stays that dark for nearly half the year.

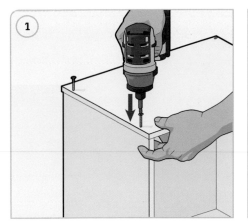

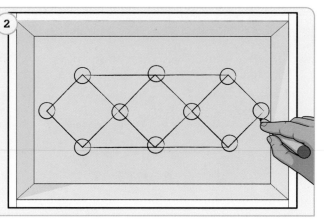

091 BUILD A LIGHT BOX

Seasonal Affective Disorder is a common form of depression experienced in the winter (or periods of reduced exposure to light), but the remedy is simple, if costly. Commercially available "full-spectrum light boxes" retail at boutique prices starting in excess of $200 and going as high as a grand. But there's no reason to shell out that kind of dough, seeing as how you're depressed enough already. Instead, you can create your own box for under $50. All you need is a wooden box (any size will do, but you're going for a combined output of 10,000 lumens, so make sure you have enough space for that many bulbs), some aluminum foil, light-bulb sockets, and a handful of CFL light bulbs.

STEP 1 Start by assembling the box (if it's not already assembled). Wood works best. You can use an old drawer from a discarded dresser if you can find one at a yard sale.

STEP 2 Draw the pattern for the bulbs on the back of the box. A diamond pattern with a socket where the lines intersect will give you three evenly spaced rows.

STEP 3 Use a circular drill bit to cut out the holes where you'll insert the bulbs.

STEP 4 Line the box with aluminum foil. Or, if you like, you can spray paint the inside with reflective, silver paint.

STEP 5 Insert the fixtures through the slots and wire them together in parallel according the manufacturer's instructions.

STEP 6 If you want to really trick out your box and make it pretty, you can attach a plywood back so the wires are covered, then mount it on the wall. Similarly, you can get a piece of plexiglass for the front. Scuff it thoroughly with sandpaper to diffuse the light.

When it's all done and ready, plug it in and sit close to the bulbs for an hour a day. Voila! Good vibes.

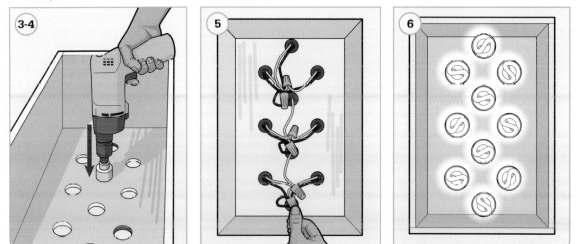

KNOW THE
TRUTH
WINTER

There are a whole host of ideas, solutions and remedies for various winter problems, but not every one of them is actually effective. Several of those ideas are just plain myths, and some of them can even be dangerous to follow. Here are a few that deserve some special attention.

GO AHEAD, LEAVE SNOW ON THE ROOF

You see it all the time—vehicles driving down city streets, highways, or mountain roads with a hefty pile of snow on the roof. And, sure, it's a lot harder to shovel off your roof than it is to scrape your windshield. So it should be fine to just make the minimal effort, scrape what's necessary, and let nature take its course with the roof layer . . . right?

FALSE In fact, along with clearing off your windows, removing the snow and ice from the roof of your vehicle after a storm is crucial to your safety and that of other drivers. It can be a pain to clear snow off the roof of a car, but you don't want a slab of ice flying off and causing an accident behind you, or sliding down your windshield, potentially causing you to crash. So take the extra time, stand on a chair if you need to, and get it done.

IT'S FINE TO FLY IN COLD AIR

It's tough to endure those brutally cold temperatures experienced near the poles during the dead of winter, and the idea of flying up higher into the atmosphere (and closer to even colder air) isn't a warming thought. Can it really be as safe as the airlines promise?

TRUE Thankfully, much to the delight of nervous fliers the world over, flying in cold weather isn't as dangerous as many people believe. Cold air is dense, which actually aids pilots in controlling their aircraft. The only thing you have to worry about when it's cold is ice forming upon the aircraft, but these days, airlines are usually extremely careful about that, so the odds you'll ever encounter an ice-related aircraft incident are minuscule.

BOILING WATER IS A GREAT DE-ICING HACK

Whether it's snow, solid ice, or a light coating of frost, it's common sense that everyone needs to clear off all of the windows in their vehicle before going out. Clearing off a little baseball-size hole in front of the driver's seat just doesn't cut it. But scraping is so tedious. If the car is parked in front of your house, in easy reach of the ol' teakettle, you have a quick-and-easy way to melt your way clear.

FALSE Stick with the ice scraper. Pouring hot water onto car windows to clear ice and snow may work ... right up until the windows shatter. But hey, at least you wouldn't have to worry about clearing them off again!

NOBODY DRIVES WELL IN THE SNOW

One of the things that residents of colder locations pride themselves on is their own perceived superior ability to drive in snowy and icy conditions. Every year when winter approaches, social media is flooded with smug declarations that people in warmer climes have nothing on the shrewd vehicular moxie of their northern counterparts. And other folks say that, really, nobody is good at navigating slippery roads and bad visibility.

TRUE People in cold climates are used to snowy weather, sure, which no doubt helps a little, but it's pretty hard to control a multi-ton vehicle with no traction. Some of the worst snow/ice-related highway pile-ups have occurred in snowy regions of the world. Don't let regional egos get in the way of safe driving.

SNOWSTORMS HAPPEN IN CYCLES

Many aspects of nature can be seen to follow patterns; having the ability to spot those patterns and learn how to react is an important part of survival. Knowing when monsoons are likely to hit, or when poisonous jellyfish show up on the beaches, are among the ways we humans avoid harm. And it just makes sense that snowstorms, like other things in nature, would also follow a predictable cycle, right?

FALSE One great storm cycle myth is that snowstorms will slam certain regions of the world on a timetable. Snowstorms just happen when they happen, depending upon the overall atmospheric setup at that moment. You can have two rough years back-to-back, and go for years without ever seeing anything more than a dusting. The idea that a blizzard occurs every five years, for instance, is usually nothing but local folklore.

SPRING

Ah, spring. It's arguably the most beautiful of the four seasons, with lovely aspects that include comfortable temperatures, ample sunshine, blooming flowers, and foliating trees; it's a period when an entire half of the world comes back to life after a long, miserable, cold winter. Spring begins when the direct rays of the sun slowly trek back across the Equator. Bright light and intense radiation from the sun warms the atmosphere and thaws the ground, allowing both land and sky to come to life in new and exciting ways.

One of the downsides to spring is that all of these beautiful changes can bring danger with them. Beautiful flowers? They bring bees. Lots of bees. Useful but terrifying bees. The surge of warmer temperatures and plentiful sunshine creates a gorgeous environment that's ripe for dangerous weather. Residents on our spaceship Earth have to stay alert for lightning, hail up to the size of softballs, winds that can shred the bark from trees, and of course, tornadoes.

The weather happens on a global scale, but it seems that disasters that happen in the United States get the lion's share of news coverage. Well, when it comes to springtime weather, there's a good reason for that: the country sweeps the board. The U.S. is uniquely positioned to see some of the most extreme weather possible, including a near-monopoly on severe thunderstorms. In fact, almost all of the tornadoes that touch down every year do so in the U.S.

Throughout the course of this chapter, we will help you identify the different ways the Earth's spring fever will try to kill you, and

give you tips on how to protect yourself and your loved ones from these unstable temper tantrums. Whether you live in Alabama, the coasts of Australia, the plains of Europe and Russia, or anywhere in between, we've got you covered as we explore the next phase of our spin around the sun.

092 BRACE FOR THUNDERSTORMS

Spring is an ideal time for thunderstorms because it features warm, moist air building up at the surface while cold winter air is still hanging around in the upper atmosphere. This sharp difference between warm below and cold above causes instability. Warm air is less dense than cold air, so the air that is warmer than its surroundings begins to rise to the top of the atmosphere like a balloon.

The rate at which the atmosphere cools with height is described by the super-geeky term "lapse rate." An environment that gets very cold very quickly with height is said to have a steep lapse rate, and it's much less stable than an environment where the air gradually warms with height. Steeper lapse rates can allow air to rise very rapidly, and these rising columns of warm, moist air can feed a thunderstorm like jet fuel. The sky's the limit with instability, and as we'll soon find out, that's a terrifying thought.

093 ALL HAIL THE SUPERCELL

Supercells are thunderstorms with a persistently rotating updraft, which is why they're sometimes called "rotating thunderstorms." These magnificent storms are rare, but can have a massive impact over a large area. Here are some common components of these beasts.

WALL CLOUDS These ominous features form in the strongest part of the updraft feeding a supercell, where warm, moist air condenses lower than the rest of the cloud base. Rotating wall clouds mean trouble brewing on the horizon—when supercells produce tornadoes, they will usually form from the wall cloud. The strongest twisters can be almost indistinguishable from their larger, parent wall clouds spinning their way through the sky.

SHELF CLOUDS These awesome structures look like long wedges attached to the leading edge of a thunderstorm. You often see a well-defined rain shaft underneath a shelf cloud, adding to their ominous appearance. Shelves can range in appearance from jagged lowerings to incredible gray waves frozen above the horizon.

MAMMATUS CLOUDS These rare but spectacular formations fill the sky around or behind intense thunderstorms. Bubbly mammatus clouds typically form high in the sky, allowing people for miles around to see them in all their glory. Mammatus clouds are so named because they resemble mammary glands, like the udders on a cow. These clouds can be subtle and hard to spot most of the time, but around powerful supercells (and especially during sunset), it's absolutely impossible to miss a sky full of bold mammatus that fill the atmosphere like heavenly bubble wrap. These clouds let you know that there's dangerous weather in the area, and pilots are taught to avoid mammatus clouds at all costs, as they indicate extreme turbulence.

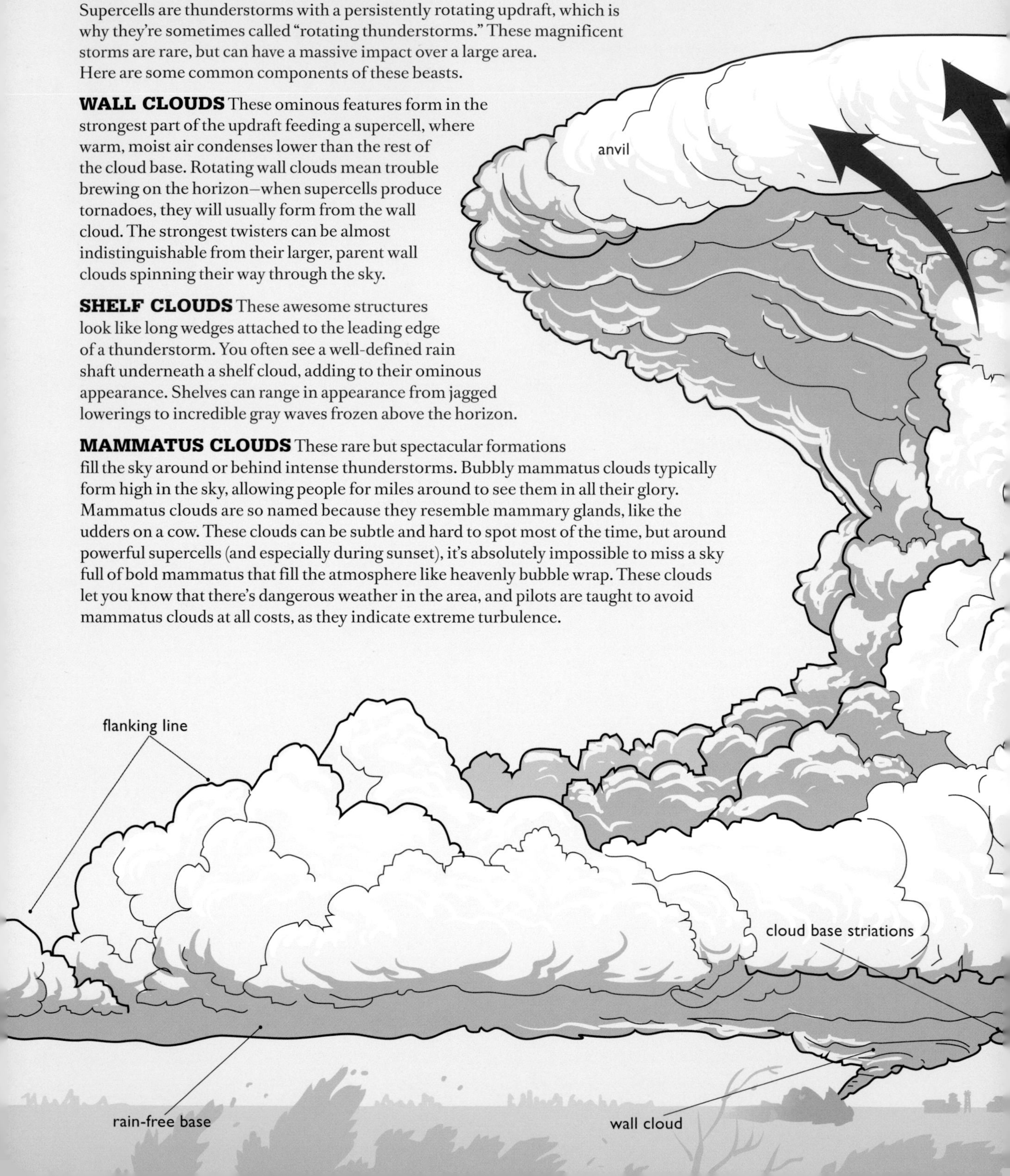

anvil

flanking line

cloud base striations

rain-free base

wall cloud

overshooting top

mammatus clouds

cumulonimbus

shelf cloud

precipitation

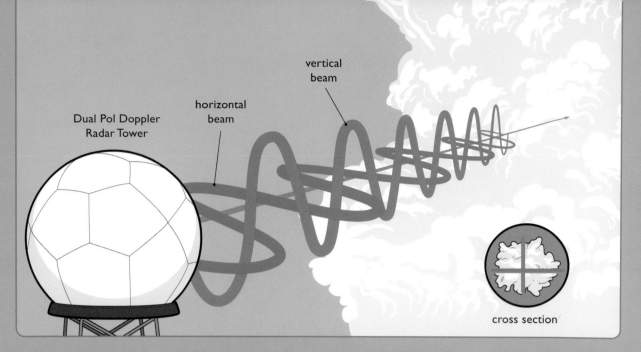

vertical beam

horizontal beam

Dual Pol Doppler Radar Tower

cross section

095 SAVE A LIFE WITH RADAR

We would be clueless without weather radar, a critical technology that has advanced by leaps and bounds since its development around World War II. After meteorologists used the Doppler effect in the 1990s in order to see winds within a thunderstorm, the next major upgrade to U.S. weather radar came in the early 2010s, with the advent of dual-polarization technology, or "dual-pol" for short.

BEAM ME UP For years, weather radar worked by sending out a single, vertically oriented beam of energy to detect precipitation. This beam allowed meteorologists to see the location, speed, and direction in which the precipitation was moving, but it didn't tell us much else.

DOUBLE YOUR DATA As you might guess from the name, dual-pol adds a second beam of energy that's oriented horizontally, resulting in a radar beam that looks like a plus sign. This dual-polar radar beam can measure the size and shape of precipitation, allowing us to differentiate between rain, snow, sleet, hail, tornado debris, and even flying creatures like bugs, birds, and bats.

SAVE THE DAY Dual-polarization isn't just cool, it's a lifesaver. At night, when it can be extremely difficult to see tornadoes with the naked eye, forecasters can use dual-pol data to confirm that there's debris in the air when it's co-located with the rotating winds detected by Doppler radar. This ability gives forecasters the confidence to say there is indeed a tornado on the ground, which in turn gives people that extra nudge to seek shelter and protect themselves.

096 SEE THE FUTURE

If you're reading this book in the year 2030, the following won't be news to you (also: greetings and apologies from the past). For the rest of us, though, we have an exciting future ahead of us when it comes to detecting storms. For years, those of us in the United States have had to wait four or five minutes between radar updates. Most of the time, that's not a problem, but that lag is critical when it comes to dangerous thunderstorms.

Around 2014, the National Weather Service upgraded its radar software with an ingenious patch to help them to alter the pattern the radar uses to sweep the skies, giving us updates twice as fast. In its fastest mode, the new patch allows radar devices around the United States to scan the horizon every two minutes, which is phenomenal when severe hail is down the street or a tornado looms around the corner.

Instead of sweeping the sky from the surface to the top of the atmosphere one level at a time like radar currently does, a new development called "phased array" weather radar will enable forecasters to scan the entire sky at once, eliminating those time-wasting individual sweeps. Phased array will let us watch thunderstorms in about as close to real time as we can get, scanning the sky and relaying data in less than one minute. This awesome technology will not only give us a better understanding of how the weather works, but also help us all survive the worst nature can throw at us.

097 LEARN A STORM'S SECRETS

Looking at the radar is a great way to know where all that precipitation is located, but sometimes we also need to use that precipitation to tell us secrets about the storm's inner workings. The two most common products available to radar users across the world are called "reflectivity" and "velocity." Reflectivity is used to make the maps you're probably used to seeing, with rainbow-colored shading that shows where the heaviest rain and snow are pouring down at the moment.

Velocity, meanwhile, tells us the speed that a storm is traveling by using the Doppler effect to determine how fast, say, a raindrop is moving. So, if the raindrop is moving east at 45 MPH, we can deduce that the winds in that region of the storm are blowing at around 45 MPH. This measure is extremely helpful in severe weather situations, especially during tornadoes.

The velocity data can rat out a tornado hiding in the rain. Most radar velocity images are shown in red and green, with reds showing wind moving away from the radar, and greens showing wind moving toward the radar. When all those red and green colors show strong winds moving in opposite directions very close to one another, you often have strong circulation in a thunderstorm or a tornado on your hands. These regions of rotation can be very subtle and hard to spot during weak tornadoes, and obvious during the most violent storms.

094 SPOT THE MOTHERSHIP

The most breathtaking photos of supercells are the result of something we like to call the "mothership," so called for its resemblance to some otherworldly craft descending from the sky to terrorize the life-forms below. Motherships are typically low-precipitation supercells with very large, strong mesocyclones (rotating updrafts) that allow you to see their immense structure without the obstruction of rain in and around the storm. These storms appear as gorgeous, layered columns of dark clouds that stand miles-tall through the atmosphere, tilting along the way.

098 HOLD THE (SQUALL) LINE

One of the most interesting types of thunderstorms is a squall line. This line of storms appears to roll across the Earth as a solid wall of strong winds and heavy rains, leaving massive damage in its wake.

A SQUALL IS BORN A squall line develops along the leading edge of a thunderstorm's outflow boundary, which acts like a mini cold front that moves along the landscape. This outflow boundary scoops up warm, unstable air out ahead of it, creating thunderstorms just behind the leading edge of the cold air. This tilted updraft can allow the storms to last for hours, traveling hundreds of miles before the boundary moves too far ahead of the convection, choking the updraft and allowing the storm to fizzle out.

DEALING DAMAGE The wind along the leading edge of a squall line can create immense damage, sometimes as bad as a tornado and over a much wider area. These winds can demolish buildings, shear the tops off of trees, knock out power to hundreds of thousands of people, and mow down entire forests like a house of cards in front of a desk fan.

SURVIVE THE STORM Unfortunately, there's not a lot you can do in the face of such power. Be sure your home is as well secured as possible and stay indoors. This is not the kind of rainstorm to run out in, no matter how scarily beautiful it seems.

099 WATCH OUT FOR GUSTNADOES

The overwhelming majority of storms that produce gusty winds and hail won't rip your house to shreds, but that doesn't mean that there aren't some pretty ugly dynamics going on when big thunderstorms line up. Every once in a while, you can experience a phenomenon known as a "gustnado," a brief, weak tornado that forms along the leading edge of a thunderstorm's outflow boundary.

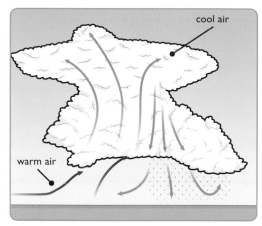

cool air

warm air

FAST AND FURIOUS How do they form? Like many neat (and dangerous) weather phenomena, gustnadoes depend on the fact that not all winds in a thunderstorm move at the same speed. This difference can cause rotations to form on either side of a blast of wind. To picture this, just think of the little swirls that form when you run your hand through the water in a swimming pool. These wind-based rotations do sometimes, in fact, end up result in fully formed tornadoes that can cause hefty damage. On the other hand, in many cases they end up producing small vortices near the ground. These little junior twisters are called gustnadoes, and they're typically small and short-lived. That said, they can be powerful for brief periods, and are capable of causing as much damage as a weak tornado.

SEEK SHELTER You probably won't hear any kind of official warning, but know that even the weakest gustnado is dangerous if it launches small objects through the air, so seek sturdy shelter if you happen upon one while admiring that sexy squall line barreling toward you on the horizon.

100 CREATE A SAFE SPACE

Going full-blown panic room or underground bunker is overkill for many—but worth considering if you live in an area that gets a lot of heavy, scary winds. Shelters built underground are the safest, but keep a couple of things in mind before you go the mole-man route. If you live in a place where soil freezes in winter, that'll stress concrete walls. Digging into bedrock? You're looking at some serious Dr. Evil fortress–type costs. And finally, look at the water table in your area. You really don't want your safe haven flooding after all that work. One good option might be using a prefab fiberglass shelter designed for underground installation, accessible by an aboveground hatch. Prices for a shelter that holds up to four adults will run you a few grand, depending on a variety of factors. How do you start planning? Consult a soil expert by searching for "geotechnical engineering" in your area.

101 FEAR THE TWISTER

No event on Earth can strike fear into your heart quite like a tornado. These testaments to nature's raw fury scream across the landscape, tearing apart everything in sight. A tornado is a rapidly spinning column of air that stretches downward from the base of a thunderstorm to the ground, potentially leaving behind a trail of destruction in its wake. The winds in a tornado can reach 300 MPH in extreme cases, but these monsters thankfully account for only a small fraction of all tornadoes that touch down.

Their very name pays tribute to the nature of these beasts—the term "tornado" most likely originated from a combination of the Spanish words *tronada* (thunderstorm) and the verb *tornar* (to turn). All tornadoes form from some type of convection, whether it's a supercell, a squall line, or the bands of rain that swirl inland as a hurricane makes landfall.

Tornadoes consist of two parts: the wind and the condensation funnel. The funnel is what you see, but it's the wind that really counts. The visible funnel that we're all familiar with is the result of low pressure within the tornado condensing water vapor in the storm's moist environment. Some tornadoes are invisible, in that they don't have a condensation funnel—in these cases, you have to look for debris swirling on the ground to confirm their existence. A rapidly rotating column of air that doesn't reach the ground is known as a funnel cloud. When the funnel cloud touches down, it becomes a tornado.

102 DON'T FALL FOR IMPOSTORS

When you see a powerful storm rolling toward you on the horizon, the different clouds, colors, and features you see can boggle your mind. One of the most unsettling sights is a black, ragged lowering extending down from the base of the storm. At a quick glance, it looks like it could be something dangerous. As it draws closer, you see that it's moving up into the storm, with more clouds filling the gap behind. It's got to be a funnel cloud, right? Not quite.

The ragged clouds you see beneath a thunderstorm are called "scud" clouds. These small cumulus clouds form underneath the base of a thunderstorm, either inside the warm, moist winds of the updraft or the condensation that forms along the leading edge of the cool, stable outflow. The winds in and around a thunderstorm can move very quickly, allowing these scud clouds to form, dissipate, and move just as fast. They are often reported as tornadoes or funnel clouds on social media, but unless you see distinct rotation in the cloud, it's just a harmless scud.

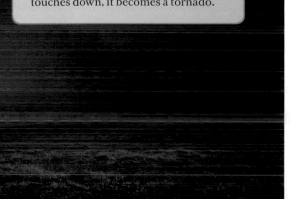

WEATHER WORLD RECORDS
LARGEST TORNADO EVER RECORDED

Oklahoma is known for its big tornadoes, but one twister that touched down in El Reno, Oklahoma, on May 31, 2013, broke the world record for largest tornado ever observed. The tornado spanned an astonishing 2.6 miles wide at one point; multiple smaller vortices within it that produced radar-estimated winds near 300 MPH. The storm killed 8 people, including several well respected storm chasers who had been caught off guard by the storm's size and erratic behavior.

103 WATCH THE BIRTH OF A MONSTER

How does a tornado form? It's one of the many questions meteorologists are still trying to answer. We're creeping closer to the answer to this one, but we're not quite there yet. Scientists began studying tornadoes in earnest back in the middle of the 20th century, but with increasingly advanced equipment, we're getting a better handle on how thunderstorms generate these volatile creatures.

MEET THE PARENTS The two most common types of tornadoes we deal with are those generated by supercells and those spawned by squall lines. Tornadoes birthed by supercells are the classic twisters that we see chasers flocking toward on the plains. The most popular theory explains that the rear-flank downdraft—the rain-cooled air that sinks around the backside of a supercell—can pull the thunderstorm's mesocyclone toward the ground, causing it to stretch and spin faster (think of an ice skater pulling her arms in) as it approaches the surface.

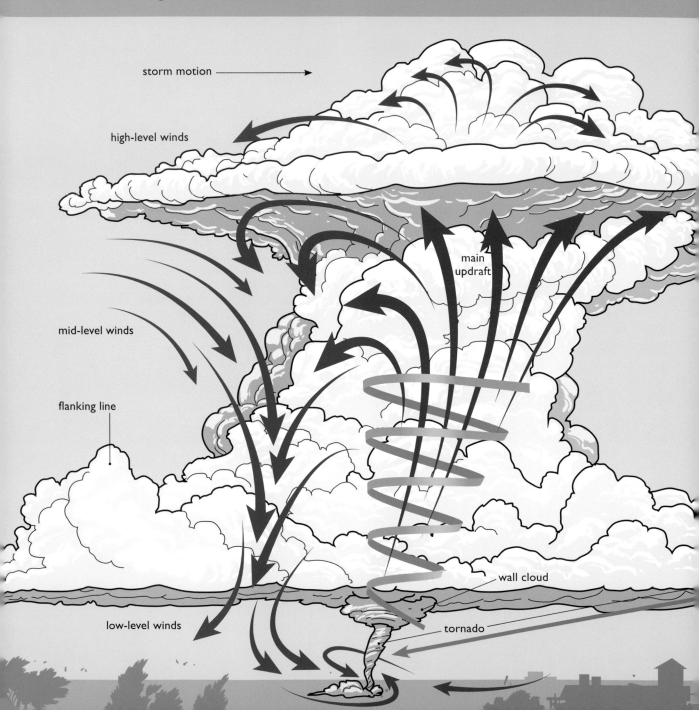

storm motion

high-level winds

main updraft

mid-level winds

flanking line

wall cloud

low-level winds

tornado

LITTLE TERRORS Tornadoes that form along the leading edge of squall lines also account for a good percentage of twisters. Many meteorologists will refer to these as weak, "spin-up" tornadoes, as they tend to be small, short-lived, and contain winds that only produce minor amounts of damage. Don't be lulled into a false sense of security by these terms. Even a small tornado can be dangerous if you're caught out unprepared and unprotected. So be prepared, even if what's coming is tiny compared to the true monster storms.

LOOK INSIDE The inner workings of a tornado are complicated, with violent winds almost always swirling counterclockwise in the Northern Hemisphere, and clockwise in the Southern. Tornadoes also have an upward component to them, with winds in the center racing skyward through the tornado and into the core of the storm. They can suck debris high into a thunderstorm, allowing it to get caught in the strong winds of the upper atmosphere; small objects like envelopes and photographs can travel hundreds of miles downwind.

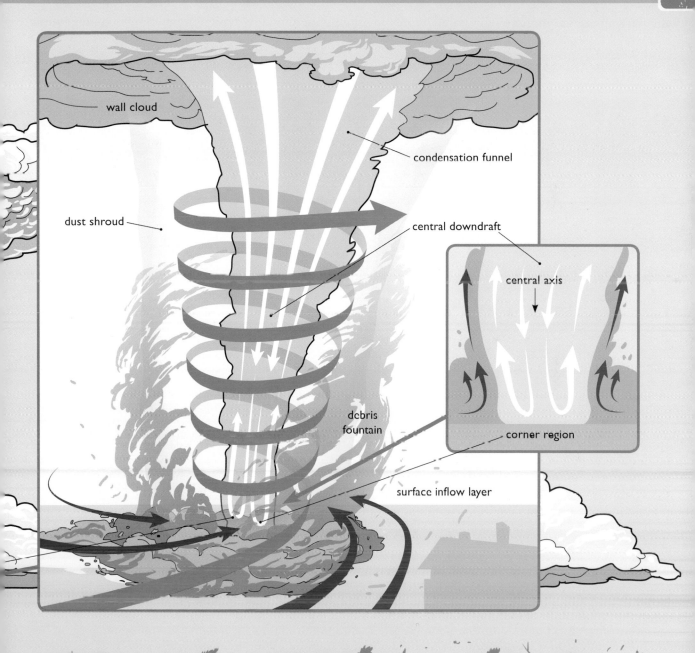

wall cloud

condensation funnel

dust shroud

central downdraft

central axis

debris fountain

corner region

surface inflow layer

104
JUDGE WHERE A TORNADO IS HEADING

If you're on the ground, staring at a tornado, you can usually tell whether it's moving to your left or right. But if a tornado looks like it's standing still, you're right in its path—and you need to get out, quick.

Tornadoes often move from southwest to northeast, so you can use a compass or a car's navigation system to avoid driving in the same direction. Of course, nothing beats the eyeball test. If you see a tornado, drive at a right angle to its path. Don't try driving directly away from the twister—that'll put you exactly in the line of danger. There's an excellent chance that the tornado will overtake you, because twisters are difficult—sometimes impossible—to outrun.

EXTREME WEATHER AROUND THE WORLD:
BANGLADESH

Of all the areas in the world prone to tornadoes on a regular basis, the most vulnerable is Bangladesh, sitting on the Ganges River Delta in southern Asia. The country's location exposes its population of more than 156 million people to violent supercells and destructive tornadoes much like those we see in places like Oklahoma and Alabama. Poor building construction and a lack of sophisticated weather monitoring and warning systems can lead to a high number of casualties during even a marginal hailstorm. As a result, Bangladesh holds the tragic distinction of having seen the world's deadliest tornado. The twister touched down in the central part of the country on April 26, 1989, killing more than 1,300 people as it demolished homes and businesses in the towns of Saturia and Daulatpur.

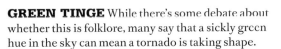
105 SPOT TORNADO WARNING SIGNS

Is that shape on the horizon an innocent cloud—or a deadly tornado? As you scan the skies, keep an eye out for these telltale signs.

SUPERCELL Look out for a looming thunderhead with a hard-edged, cauliflower look. This is a supercell: a dangerous formation that can produce interior winds of up to 170 MPH.

WALL CLOUD These look dense and, well, sort of like a wall, with clearly defined edges.

GREEN TINGE While there's some debate about whether this is folklore, many say that a sickly green hue in the sky can mean a tornado is taking shape.

FUNNEL CLOUD A needle-like formation that's descending from a cloud's base indicates its rotation. When a funnel cloud touches the ground, it becomes a tornado—luckily most never touch down.

STRANGE SOUNDS Listen up for any sounds like swarming bees or a waterfall—these may be an approaching twister you're hearing. If your ears pop, there's been a drop in air pressure, which is another danger sign.

Supercell

Green Tinge

Wall Cloud

Funnel Cloud

106 KNOW WHEN TO WORRY

Almost more important than knowing where to seek shelter and what to do when a tornado is barreling toward you is to know in advance when one could potentially bear down on your location. Thanks to Doppler weather radar and dramatic advances in forecasting, meteorologists can typically warn residents of a potential tornado 15 or more minutes before it strikes. The lead time is critical, as it allows you to put your safety plan into action.

TORNADO WATCH This type of alert means that conditions are favorable for the development of severe thunderstorms that are capable of producing tornadoes. Tornado watches are typically issued hours in advance of the arrival of thunderstorms, and they are meant to put residents on alert to pay hawk-like attention to the latest developments and updates.

TORNADO WARNING This stronger alert indicates that a tornado has been spotted or Doppler weather radar detects strong rotation that could lead to the imminent development of a tornado. Unlike a tornado watch, a tornado warning means the twister has touched down; you are in immediate danger and need to take swift action to save your life and the lives of those around you.

Tornado warnings typically have a lead time of about 15 minutes, but this can be much shorter (or much longer) depending on the situation.

Meteorologists are experimenting with different terminology for tornado warnings to convey the relative severity of a situation. If spotters report that a violent tornado is moving into a populated area, meteorologists will upgrade a tornado warning to a tornado emergency, in an attempt to give people extra motivation to take lifesaving measures. This exceedingly rare designation was developed by the National Weather Service in Norman, Oklahoma, on May 3, 1999, when a violent EF-5 tornado tore through the southern suburbs of Oklahoma City, killing 36 people.

107 AVOID TORNADO ALLEY

The United States is ground zero for the most violent tornadoes in the world; in fact, more than three-quarters of all the tornadoes that touch down every year occur in the United States. Warm, moist air pumping in from the Gulf of Mexico and cold winds aloft blowing in from the west often create the perfect mixture of moisture, instability, and wind shear for big twisters.

SOUTHERN EXPOSURE Tornado Alley is a swath of the central U.S. that serves as a breeding ground for tornado outbreaks. Its flat terrain and favorable storm tracks allow Tornado Alley to see violent twisters on a fairly regular basis. Another hot spot for tornadoes is called "Dixie Alley," a region stretching from central Mississippi through northern Alabama and southeastern Tennessee. The worst tornado outbreak in U.S. history unfolded in Dixie Alley on April 27, 2011, when 211 tornadoes killed 354 people and injured thousands more.

ACROSS THE COUNTRY Twisters can and have occurred in all 50 states. Some regions of the country see few tornadoes, such the deep Appalachian and Rocky Mountains, as well as portions of the West Coast, but they aren't completely immune to these rotating windstorms. The state with the fewest tornadoes is Alaska; due to its cool and stable weather, and few residents around to see the rare twisters that do happen, only four tornadoes have been reported there since 1950.

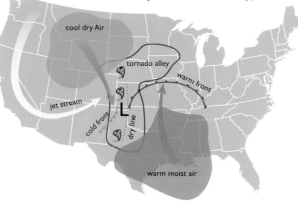

KNOW THE TRUTH
TORNADOES

Everyone who grew up in an area susceptible to tornadoes has heard at least one of the myths regarding these storms and how to survive them. Most of these stories began in an era when we knew very little or nothing about how tornadoes form or how they manage to do things such as destroy entire buildings in a matter of seconds. Here are some commonly circulated factoids about tornadoes—some true, and some a complete load of debris.

OPEN THE WINDOWS

The news says a tornado is barreling right for your town. Quick! What do you do? Depending on whatever you were taught when you were a child, your first instinct might be to open up your house's windows to equalize the air pressure between the outdoors and your house. That's true, right?

FALSE It isn't really the extreme pressure difference that destroys your house, it's the wind. In fact, opening the windows will make it easier for the tornado's wind and debris to move through your house and tear it apart, thus posing a grave threat to your safety.

CHECK THAT TREE

When we teach children about the power of these devastating storms, one of the first things that we do to catch their attention is tell them that in a tornado's wind, even a tiny wooden splinter can slice through a brick wall like a hot knife through soft butter.

TRUE Even the smallest debris lofted into the air by a tornado travels at mind-boggling speeds, and it can do some pretty gnarly damage once it reaches its final destination. It's not uncommon to see plywood lanced through concrete curbs or full-grown trees after a particularly violent twister.

GREEN'S THE KEY

The sky often takes on an unsettling look right before a thunderstorm engulfs you. Survivors of tornadoes frequently note in documentaries and reports that the sky would turn a sickly dark green before the storm hit—a common refrain out on the Great Plains.

FALSE The sky does turn an ugly green shade before a big storm, but it isn't always a herald of tornadoes. The sky likely turns green because sunlight has to filter through a miles-thick layer of rain and clouds before it reaches the ground, scattering green light much as it does in a deep lake. Storms strong enough to produce tornadoes usually bring copious rain and hail. Thus, there's a correlation, but not 100%.

IT COULD SKIP MY HOUSE

Another scary tale that tornado veterans like to tell frightened newbies is that violent tornadoes have no rhyme or reason, skipping over one house while demolishing the house next door.

TRUE This idea is at least partially true. Large tornadoes can also have smaller suction vortices embedded within them — think of two or three smaller, stronger tornadoes within the larger tornadic circulation. All of these suction vortices are small enough that they can cause the total destruction of one house, and skip the home next door. That house might still get a bit beat up, but it could see much less damage than the unfortunate Joneses.

IT CAN'T HAPPEN HERE

We've all heard someone proudly assert that they're immune to tornadoes because they live next to a mountain, river, lake, or in an apartment in some swanky downtown neighborhood, right?

FALSE Those folks are wrong. Very wrong. Mountainous regions have a moderating effect on the conditions that produce large tornadoes, but mountain communities are by no means immune to tornadoes. Tornadoes also have no trouble crossing bodies of water. Twisters aren't fazed by cities, either. The densely populated cores of New York City, Atlanta, Salt Lake City, Nashville, and Miami have all been hit by tornadoes in recent years.

108 RATE THE FURY

Attempting to directly measure the winds in a tornado is a dangerous and sometimes impossible task. The best way to estimate a tornado's strength is to study the damage it leaves behind. Dr. Theodore Fujita was a world-renowned meteorologist who pioneered tornado research, and he developed the Fujita Scale (now the Enhanced Fujita or EF) which uses the damage caused to different types of buildings as a way to estimate a tornado's wind speed at a particular location. By studying the damage caused to a well-built, wood-frame house, for instance, you can get a pretty accurate measure of how strong a tornado was.

EF-0
SEVERITY: Minor
RELATIVE FREQUENCY: Most common
ESTIMATED WIND GUSTS: 65–85 MPH
DAMAGE EXPECTED: Shingles removed and minor roof damage possible; gutters and vinyl siding damaged. Tree branches and limbs felled, weak trees knocked over.

EF-1
SEVERITY: Moderate
RELATIVE FREQUENCY: Common
ESTIMATED WIND GUSTS: 86–110 MPH
DAMAGE EXPECTED: Windows broken, mobile or prefabricated homes severely damaged. Significant roof damage to well-built homes.

EF-2
SEVERITY: Considerable
RELATIVE FREQUENCY: Common
ESTIMATED WIND GUSTS: 111–135 MPH
DAMAGE EXPECTED: Roofs torn off; structural damage to homes possible. Mobile or prefabricated homes destroyed. Cars overturned.

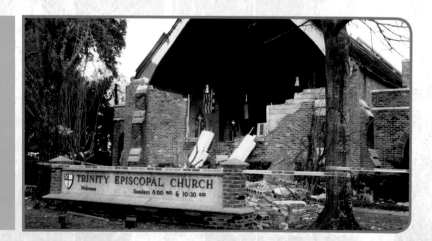

EF-3

SEVERITY: Severe
RELATIVE FREQUENCY: Infrequent
ESTIMATED WIND GUSTS: 136–165 MPH
DAMAGE EXPECTED: Possible significant, irreparable damage to well-built structures. Top floors sheared off homes and businesses. Cars tossed through the air.

EF-4

SEVERITY: Extreme
RELATIVE FREQUENCY: Rare
ESTIMATED WIND GUSTS: 165–200 MPH
DAMAGE EXPECTED: Commercial buildings and homes leveled. Reinforced structures such as schools and prisons sustain serious damage.

EF-5

SEVERITY: Catastrophic
RELATIVE FREQUENCY: Exceptionally rare
ESTIMATED WIND GUSTS: 201+ MPH
DAMAGE EXPECTED: Most buildings scrubbed to their foundation. Steel storage tanks may be sheared from their bolts. Vehicles mangled beyond recognition. Trees debarked. Grass and roads scoured from the earth.

109 DON'T GO MOBILE

Every time a tornado whirls through the area, you flip on the news and hear a tragic story about how a family was killed when their mobile home was swept away in the fierce winds.

UNDERSTAND THE DANGER The two main weaknesses of these abodes are the open space under the trailer and the lightweight building materials. The space underneath can allow wind to blow under the trailer, which can end up flipping it or lifting it into the air. The lightweight construction that makes these dwellings mobile also enables the tornado to move them, occasionally shredding them into tiny pieces. Even small tornadoes can destroy tied-down mobile homes, and even the best-built and most modern of mobile homes and trailers aren't able to handle the high winds and incredible wrenching forces.

BE VIGILANT Mobile-home dwellers need to take an extra level of precautions when heavy weather threatens. Be ready to go before the tornado warning sounds—preferably even before the watch does. That mens watching the news on TV or online, and being ready to get up and go before the last minute. Better to run for town unnecessarily than to get caught in a whirling deathtrap.

GET TO SAFETY If you're caught in a mobile home during a tornado warning, your best bet is to quickly evacuate to a sturdier building for shelter.

110 SHELTER IN PLACE, PROPERLY

When a tornado threatens, the simplest advice is to get yourself to the safest and sturdiest spot that's close and easy to reach. No matter where you end up sheltering, use this basic body-protecting technique: Crouch down low with your face downward. Cover your head with your hands, or throw on a sports helmet for protection against head injury if at all possible. Wrap up in blankets or sleeping bags to pad against bodily injury, or flop a mattress on top of you for storm debris protection.

BASEMENT REFUGE If you're in a house with a basement, go down there and crawl under something sturdy. This could be a heavy table, a work bench, a mattress, or the like. Stay keenly aware of the position of heavy objects (like refrigerators, waterbeds, pianos, etc.) on the floor above the basement, and don't hang out under those spots. Also, avoid windows and sliding glass doors, as well as chimneys (which might collapse).

SMALL-SPACE SAFETY If you're in a space that has no basement, the first rule is to stay away from the windows. Go to a bathroom, closet, or a space under the stairs on the lowest floor. Failing that, get to an interior hallway with no windows. Jumping into a bathtub may offer partial protection, but cover up with some sort of thick padding, like a mattress or several blankets.

OUT IN PUBLIC
If you're in a church, theater, mall, or large store, get to shelter as quickly as you can, such as an interior bathroom, a storage room, or other small enclosure away from any windows. If you're at school, follow the staff's instructions.

111 RIDE IT OUT IN THE OPEN

There is no good way to survive in the open, which is why paying attention to weather forecasts is so crucial. That said, if you *do* get caught outdoors and there is no sturdy shelter within running distance. These instructions (and a lot of luck) may help. Lie face down in a low area. Protect the back of your head with your arms and any extra clothing you have. Don't try to hold onto a tree, or shelter near other seemingly solid objects. They may be blown onto you, or you may be scooped up and hurled at them.

EXTREME WEATHER HISTORY:
1925 TRI-STATE TORNADO

People who woke up across the central United States on the morning of March 18, 1925, had little warning of the danger in store for them later that day. A significant tornado outbreak that afternoon would lead to the single deadliest tornado in the country's history, and one with the longest track ever recorded.

The tornado touched down in southeastern Missouri near the town of Ellington, and continued northeast over the next three-and-a-half hours across Illinois until it finally lifted in southwestern Indiana, a continuous 235-mile path. There is some debate over whether the tornado was truly one tornado or a family of tornadoes that touched down one after the other. Many reports indicate that the storm's path of damage was continuous, but the lack of advanced tracking methods (along with the almost 100 years that have elapsed since) make it hard to know the answer for sure.

When the tornado finally lifted in Indiana, the damage it left behind was historic. The storm injured thousands of people and ultimately claimed 695 lives, which is the highest death toll from a single tornado in United States history. As staggering and tragic as the death toll was, it could have been much higher. We take for granted our advanced forecast and warning systems today, but the science of meteorology was still budding in the 1920s. Many residents affected by the tornado did not realize that it was coming until it was on top of them. Given this, along with the fact that entire towns were destroyed—this storm demolished more than 15,000 buildings along its path—this tragically high death toll is surprisingly low, given the incredible confluence of events that produced this unprecedented tornado.

112 STAY OUT OF THE CORNER

One of the oldest surviving tornado myths is that the safest part of your home during a tornado is the southwest corner of the structure. This myth cropped up due to the fact that classic tornadoes spawned by supercell thunderstorms typically move from the southwest to the northeast. This isn't always true—tornadoes can come from any direction. The safest place in your home is underground or in an interior room. The corner of the building doesn't matter as much as whether you're safe from the wind; you should always try to get underground or in an interior room during a tornado. The more walls and distance you put between yourself and the flying debris and wind, the higher your chances of survival.

113 KNOW THE ODDS

I was terrified of tornadoes when I was a child—even in middle school, I would go hang out with the neighbors when dangerous weather threatened and I was home alone. It's natural and even healthy to fear these beastly whirlwinds, but for as much play as they get in the news, they're not as common as you might think.

Let's take a look at the numbers. From the Florida Keys to the Puget Sound, the United States can see more than 100,000 individual thunderstorms every year. The National Weather Service estimates that only five percent of all the thunderstorms that form in the country produce severe weather, and only about one percent of all thunderstorms go on to produce a tornado. Even if a thousand tornado-producing thunderstorms sounds like a lot, consider the fact that most tornadoes are only a few hundred feet wide and last for ten minutes at the most. That's a relatively small patch of real estate that's affected by these vortices.

If it's strength you're worried about, consider the fact that only 0.1% of all tornadoes that have formed within the United States produced EF-5 damage—the highest rating on the scale used to estimate the intensity of a tornado. The overwhelming majority of tornadoes (close to 90%) are between EF-0 and EF-2 intensity; this is strong enough to pose a serious threat to people who aren't protected, but is hardly enough to scour homes down to their foundations.

In short, it's always wise to prepare for the worst-case scenario, but the odds are relatively low that you'll ever directly experience a tornado in your lifetime.

114 SURVIVE ON THE ROAD

Sheltering in vehicles is a very risky gambit in a tornado, as cars can be tumbled or thrown by a strong twister. It really boils down to a choice of similar perils. If you see a tornado while you're driving in a car, and it's far away and you have open road ahead, then you might be able to outrun it by driving at a right angle to the tornado's path (if you can tell what that is). Of course, the smarter choice is to seek shelter indoors or underground, if at all possible.

If you're caught in a vehicle and cannot drive, the best option is usually to abandon the vehicle.

You're probably safer when lying in a ditch than you are sitting in the car. If you do decide to stay in the car, or you don't have time to run to a ditch, keep your seat belt fastened, cover your head with your hands, and use a jacket, coat, or some other covering to protect you from flying debris. The vehicle will be safer on a lower road level than a higher one or on a bridge.

That said, do not head for an overpass, no matter whether you've seen any movie characters or people in documentaries who do and live to tell about it. Aside from flying through the air, this is the worst place to be in a tornado. Let me be clear: **It is not safe to take shelter under an overpass during a tornado.** Overpasses do not provide protection—in fact, the air squeezing into the tight spaces under an overpass actually increases the tornado's wind speed, increasing the chance that you'll get sucked out or pelted with debris.

115 STUDY YOUR TORNADOES

Tornadoes are versatile forces that can manifest in various different shapes and sizes. One of the worst misconceptions people have about these whirlwinds is that smaller tornadoes aren't as dangerous as larger ones. Most tornadoes are on the weaker side and only stretch a few hundred feet wide, but size doesn't indicate intensity. It doesn't take a big tornado to loft debris fast enough to seriously injure or kill you.

TYPE OF TORNADO	DESCRIPTION	KNOW THE FACTS
ROPE	As its name suggests, looks like a rope twisting and turning through the sky.	Rope tornadoes are commonly seen toward the end of a twister's life cycle, when the vortex is losing the battle against more stable air. Some of the most spectacular storm pictures ever captured show rope tornadoes that perform intricate twists and zigzags through the sky.
CONE	A wide vortex near the base of the cloud, slowly slimming down to a point at the surface.	The most commonly depicted tornado shape. The base of cone tornadoes is often obscured by flying debris and dust, making the base appear larger than it is. These tornadoes can range from weak to intense.
STOVEPIPE	Smooth, uniform columns stretching from the ground to the thunderstorm.	Much like their conic counterparts, they have a wide range of intensities, and the base can look larger due to swirling debris.
WEDGE 	Gigantic, roaring masses of fury that can grow one mile wide or even larger.	The strongest tornadoes ever recorded were all wedge tornadoes, and they can level entire neighborhoods in seconds. Wedges aren't always one single vortex, either—these monsters often have numerous smaller vortices circling around inside of them like the matryoshka doll from hell. These mini-tornadoes are called suction vortices, and they're usually responsible for the most severe damage in a large wedge tornado.

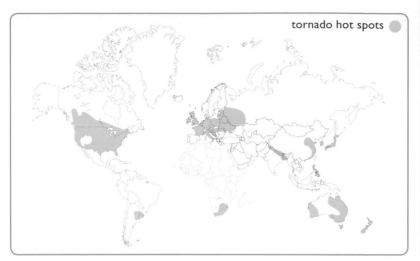

tornado hot spots ●

116 SEE A WORLD OF TROUBLE

Thanks to weather trends mixed with a dollop of cultural egotism, it seems like we only ever hear about tornadoes that form in the United States. There are some other hot spots for activity beyond our fruited plains. As we noted a few pages back, Bangladesh is particularly vulnerable, but you'll find twisters around the globe.

Tornado activity is possible almost anywhere in Europe during the stormy spring and summer months—northern Italy and portions of Germany and Poland often see several violent tornadoes a year.

South Africa and eastern Australia can also see a handful of raucous supercells every year, spawning picturesque tornadoes that tear through a mostly unpopulated landscape. Even Japan is also known to see a couple of tornadoes every year, which is especially dangerous given the high population densities in many of its cities.

117 WATCH THE CRITTERS

A lot of folklore tells us that we can predict weather trends by watching animal behavior. Is there anything to it? Scientists claim it's likely that some animals are sensitive to environmental changes we can't perceive and thus do, in fact, have an early warning system for some heavy weather.

UNDER PRESSURE It does seem to be the case that birds and some insects may sense barometric pressure changes, or even hear sound cues outside human hearing, and be able to tell that a hurricane or other major storm is coming.

BIRD WATCHING In short, if the flying critters in an area all seem to be seeking shelter, they might be trying to tell you something. Be alert to the signs around you.

DENNIS DEBUNKS:
RUBBER SHOES KEEP YOU SAFE

One common misconception about being outdoors in a lightning storm is that you can insulate yourself against danger by wearing rubber shoes. Sorry, but the fact is that "keep the rubber side down" is for motorcycles, not outdoorspeople. If you're outside in a storm, you're at risk. So put down the fishing pole, stop the hunt, and get away from that campsite if you possibly can. Mother Nature always wins, and when the skies open up, she's packing a lot of firepower.

118 CAMP SAFELY

When spring rolls around, many of us just can't wait to get out into the great outdoors. After being cooped up inside a winterized home for the past several months, the warming trends herald an opportunity for a great escape. However, that stampede of campers, hunters, and anglers into the wilderness does bring along with it some increased risk. Thunderstorms and lightning can pose some real risks to campers, and most of us are loath to cancel a trip, leaving us exposed to the elements. Here are some pointers to help keep you safe.

GIVE UP EASILY When you hear thunder, it's time to move indoors. While no one wants to cancel an activity, by the time we hear thunder approaching, we're already within reach of a lightning strike. So act accordingly, and live to camp another day.

GET IN THE CAR If it's too late to ditch the trip, you'll at least want to stay out of your tent until the storm blows over. Especially out in the open, tents can actually attract a lightning strike. You're better off getting into your vehicle to ride out the storm.

AVOID SOME SHELTERS Don't just head for a rain shelter. Many campgrounds will provide roofed structures that are great at keeping you dry. But don't think that they'll protect you from lightning. Quite the opposite. You want to get into a fully enclosed structure or an RV with the windows closed for maximum protection.

119 MAKE WATERPROOF MATCHES

One of the biggest issues with surviving outdoors is staying warm and dry. In the event of a thunderstorm, a lot of vital supplies, like matches, are at risk of getting soaked. Before you head out on a camping or fishing trip, here's a quick and easy way to create a survival match that will light up even in the wettest and wildest conditions. Use kitchen matches, the old-fashioned matchsticks with a sulfur head.

STEP 1 Cut a 3- or 4-inch strip of paper towel that is the same length as the matchstick.

STEP 2 Place the matchstick on the paper towel's edge with its head exposed, and roll the stick tightly inside.

STEP 3 Light a tea candle. Once it's melted completely, blow out the candle, then dip both ends of the matchstick into the wax. Make sure the entirety of the paper towel and the match head are coated in wax.

STEP 4 Allow the match- to dry, then pack carefully in a waterproof container.

At this point, you've got a waterproof match that will survive complete submersion in water. Before striking the match, just use your thumbnail to remove the wax coating from the striker. When you do strike the match, the wax coating and paper towel will allow the match to act like a candle, lasting long enough to make sure your fire gets started before the match burns out.

120
KNOW YOUR LIGHTNING

No two bolts of lightning are the same. Sometimes, lightning won't even be a bolt at all. There are a variety of different types of lightning that you may might encounter on your adventures, whether they take you to the top of the world or to your cubicle.

Cloud-to-Cloud Lightning

	INTRA-CLOUD (IC) LIGHTNING	CLOUD-TO-CLOUD (CC) LIGHTNING	CLOUD-TO-GROUND (CG) LIGHTNING	DRY LIGHTNING	BOLT FROM THE BLUE
RISK TO LIFE	Minimal	Minimal	Severe	Severe	Severe
CHARACTERISTICS	A flash of lightning that travels inside a single cloud.	A flash of lightning that travels between two different clouds. Crackling thunder possible.	A brilliant bolt of lightning that extends from clouds to the ground, branching out, forking, and zigzagging along its path.	Dry lightning is cloud-to-ground lightning that occurs in a thunderstorm with little or no precipitation.	Cloud-to-ground lightning that strikes with no warning, often under clear or blue skies; can come from a thunderstorm 20 or more miles away from you.
DANGERS	The dangers of IC and CC lightning are fairly minimal to most of us mere mortals, but aircraft are frequently (and harmlessly) struck by lightning bolts that occur within and between storm clouds.		Cloud-to-ground lightning can cause damage, fires, and even human and animal injury or death.	Dry lightning is a major problem in grasslands and forests, where it can lead to raging wildfires without rainfall to help put out the flames. It can also pose a risk to humans who might be caught outdoors without safe shelter.	Since people do not usually seek shelter until the storm is on top of them, bolts from the blue are one of the most dangerous types of lightning due to their surprise factor.

Cloud-to-Ground Lightning

"Heat" Lightning

Intra-Cloud Lightning

"HEAT" LIGHTNING	NEGATIVE LIGHTNING	POSITIVE LIGHTNING	BALL LIGHTNING
Minimal	Severe	Extreme	Minimal due to its rarity, but there's not enough research to say for sure.
The phrase "heat lightning" is both popular as well as a misnomer—the term is applied to a thunderstorm that is too distant for you to hear thunder, but you still see flashes in the clouds on the horizon.	Negative lightning is the most common type of lightning that we experience, with the stroke originating from the negatively charged base of a thunderstorm.	The most intense form of lightning, these bolts form from the positively charged regions of the upper thunderstorm. They carry at least ten times more power than negative lightning, and form the majority of bolts from the blue.	Ball lightning is a rare phenomenon that isn't very well understood. Most reports describe ball lightning as a floating orb between the size of an apple and a car, lasting several seconds before finally dissipating.
Lightning that is far away is generally no cause for concern, but beware the bolt from the blue.	The risks of negative lightning are the same risks from cloud to ground lightning—it can seriously injure or kill you if it strikes you or something nearby. a Even if you don't die, the lingering physical side effects of a lightning strike can be debilitating.	Positive bolts of lightning can cause major damage, fires, and are especially lethal if you happen to be struck by one. These very highly energized bolts, while rare, may pose a threat to aircraft as they were discovered and researched after most aircraft safety measures were created.	Eyewitness accounts of ball lightning indicate that it has erratic behavior, and can either pass through objects like walls and windows or cause them to burst into flames. Either way, in the unlikely event you encounter ball lightning, it's best that you stay away from it.

121 GET A CHARGE

When you put on a pair of socks and run across the carpet on a cold winter's day, you can cause a nice, loud shock when you turn off a light (or carry out your evil urges by zapping someone). This static electricity results from an imbalance of positive and negative electrical charges. When you walk across the room and switch off the light, the negative charges on your hands leap to the positively charged metal screws or plate around the switch, resulting in that shock we all know and hate.

WHAT IT IS Lightning is a type of static discharge that results from different electrical charges in the atmosphere and the surface of the Earth. The most widely accepted theory for why lightning happens is that this electrostatic charge is built up between ice crystals in strong storms, thus allowing positive and negative charges to separate from each other. There are different layers of electrical charges within a cloud, but the most familiar setup is with a layer of negative charges at the base of the cloud, and a layer of positive charges on the ground. The discharge occurs as a flash of lightning, one in a long series of futile attempts by nature to achieve balance in the universe.

HOW IT WORKS Very much like a college student, electricity will try to find the easiest way for it to do something, thus taking the path of least resistance. Lightning can strike anything outdoors (and sometimes even indoors), but it prefers taller objects, which is why it's important for you to stay away from tall things like trees, flagpoles, or power lines if you're caught out in the open during a thunderstorm.

122 FLY THE UNFRIENDLY SKIES

Modern airplanes are designed to withstand most lightning strikes. Almost every commercial airliner is struck by lightning at least once in its lifetime—much more often for planes that regularly fly through stormy regions. The bolt of lightning typically hits the airframe, following along the skin to the other end of the aircraft, where it branches off and dissipates without incident.

The greatest danger to an aircraft when lightning strikes is combustible vapor inside the plane's fuel tanks. This was a major issue in the early days of aviation when we were still learning about the risks and hazards of flight. One notorious incident occurred in December 1963, when a Boeing 707 crashed on its route from Baltimore to Philadelphia after lightning ignited fuel vapors in its tank, causing the aircraft to explode and fall to the ground.

While regulations vary around the world, many commercial airlines in the United States are now required to pump inert (non-reactive) gas into the fuel tanks of their larger aircraft to prevent fuel vapors from igniting and thus potentially causing an explosion. So, the next time that you fly through a heavy thunderstorm and see a lightning flash outside your window, take comfort in the fact that the plane is designed to brush off these bolts and safely carry you onward to your destination.

123 PREDICT A STRIKE

The sudden jolt of a loud crack of thunder is as startling as it is exhilarating. But why does it come from? Basically, lightning is extremely hot—in fact, it can reach temperatures almost ten times hotter than the surface of the sun (which is about 9,900°F, if you were wondering). Warm air expands when it's heated, but when such an intensely hot bolt of lightning slices through the sky, it causes this air to instantly heat up, forcing it to rapidly expand. This explosive expansion of the air creates a sonic boom, which is where that familiar rumble of thunder comes from.

You can use science to your advantage to know how close a lightning strike is to your location. When you see a flash of lightning, start counting the seconds that elapse between the flash and the moment you hear the clap of thunder. Divide that number by five, and you'll have a rough approximation of how far away the lightning strike occurred, in miles. For instance, if you see lightning and count 15 seconds before you hear the thunder, the lightning strike was about 3 miles away. This system isn't precise, but it's a good way to use the speed of sound to your advantage in a survival situation (or just for fun).

Bottom line? If you can see lightning *and* hear thunder, you're close enough to be struck. Get indoors as quickly as you can.

124 AVOID LIGHTNING HOT SPOTS

Thunderstorms are prolific lightning producers and they account for almost all of the lightning seen throughout the world. The globe sees more than one billion lightning strikes per year, spread out across almost every single bit of land except for the Arctic and Antarctic Circles, where even the summer air there is usually too cold and stable for thunderstorms to develop.

While the frequent thunderstorms in Florida make it the most lightning-prone region in North America, it's far from the lightning capital of the world. Areas around the equator—where it's fairly hot and humid the whole year—can see thunderstorms almost every day. Venezuela's Lake Maracaibo (pictured above) is noted for its "Catatumbo Lightning," where thunderstorms develop every night near the mouth of the lake for more than half the year, producing an incredible lightning show that can zap the surrounding terrain with hundreds of bolts each night.

The area of the world that sees the highest number of lightning strikes annually is the rainforests and savanna of central Africa, with the most strikes occurring in eastern Democratic Republic of Congo, near the country's border with Uganda and Rwanda. The equatorial areas of Africa, along with the islands of south Asia and the rainforests of South America, are home to the most numerous flashes of lightning on Earth.

125

UNDERSTAND THE DEADLY FORCE

Largely due to advanced detection methods, along with fewer people spending time outdoors, the number of lightning deaths in the United States has dropped from more than 400 in 1942 to fewer than two dozen in 2013.

DEATH FROM ABOVE Bolts of lightning are powerful forces, in terms of electricity as well as the heat they can generate. A direct strike by a lightning bolt can create such a strong electrical pulse inside a human body that the heart can seize and send the victim into cardiac arrest; Unless they receive adequate medical attention immediately, this can be fatal.

CLOSE ENCOUNTERS
Lightning that misses a person but hits a nearby object is still potentially deadly—the electricity can still travel through the ground and injure or kill anyone nearby. A significant portion of lightning victims are either injured or killed when lightning hits a nearby object like a tree or pole, then sends a charge through the ground that can reach bystanders.

AFTERSHOCK The vast majority of people who are struck by lightning are fortunate enough to live through the encounter, but it won't exactly be smooth sailing for any survivors. Side effects from a brush with lightning can be brutal, inflicting excruciating amounts of physical and mental pain on the survivor. Common lingering effects include nerve injuries; issues with vision, hearing, and balance; and seizures, headaches, and mental and cognitive impairment. Even if a person is lucky enough to survive a lightning strike, the damage can last for the rest of his or her life.

126 HELP SOMEONE STRUCK BY LIGHTNING

Contrary to popular belief (and millions of cartoons), lightning victims usually aren't badly burned. You're more likely to end up grappling with these symptoms instead.

A STOPPED HEART The primary cause of death for lightning-strike victims is cardiac arrest. It's also common for the strike to damage the lungs, so a victim may stop breathing. If you know CPR, then chest compressions are the way to go (A).

PARALYSIS The victim may not be able to move or speak, due to an acute form of paralysis that's unique to lightning strikes—and thankfully temporary. Do your best to keep him or her reassured and warm until medical assistance arrives (B).

MISSING CLOTHES A strike can blow off your clothes. A blanket will help with warmth—and modesty (C).

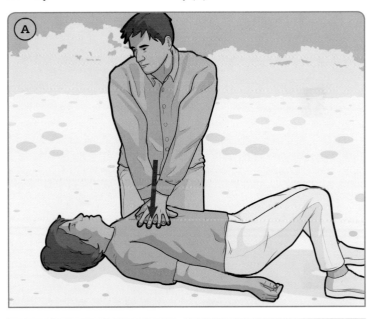
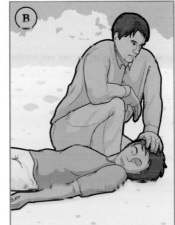

127 SURVIVE A LIGHTNING STRIKE

There are lots of snappy sayings to help you remember lightning safety: When the thunder roars, go indoors! If you can see it, flee it! But what do you do when you're caught outdoors with virtually nowhere to hide? The National Outdoor Leadership Schools, or NOLS, and other experts recommend the following.

IF YOU ARE CLOSE TO YOUR VEHICLE OR AN ENCLOSED STRUCTURE Get inside it, no matter what it is—your car, a house, a barn. Open structures such as picnic shelters will provide little to no protection.

IF YOU ARE CAMPING Avoid open fields and ridge tops during seasons when thunderstorms are prevalent. Stay away from fence lines, metal, and tall, isolated trees. Tents provide no protection. If you are in dangerous open terrain during a thunderstorm, leave the tent and assume the "lightning crunch" position (described in the last paragraph).

IF YOU ARE IN OPEN COUNTRY Avoid the high ground and contact with dissimilar objects, such as water and land, boulders and land, or single trees and land. Head for ditches, gullies, or low ground. Have your group spread out at least 50 feet apart and assume the "lightning crunch."

IF YOU ARE ON THE WATER Head inside the boat cabin, which offers a safer environment. Stay off the radio unless it is an emergency. Drop anchor and get as low in the boat as possible. If you're in a canoe on open water, get as low in the canoe as possible and as far as possible from any metal object. If shore only offers rocky crags and tall, isolated trees, stay in the boat.

IF YOU CANNOT FIND SHELTER Some experts believe that the "lightning crouch" provides little to no protection from a direct or close strike, but you may feel like any action is better than none. Stand on an insulated pad or bag of clothes. Do not stand on packs; the metal in the frames and zippers could increase chances of a lightning strike. Put your feet together and balance on the balls of your feet. Squat low, wrap your arms around your legs, tuck your head, close your eyes, and cover your ears. Maintain the position until danger passes.

KNOW THE TRUTH
LIGHTNING

Just like almost everything else in the world, we've developed myths over the course of time to help explain things we know very little about. Lightning is a hazard that we've had to deal with since the beginning of civilization, and the number of myths about this electrifying force grows larger by the year. Here are some commonly circulated factoids about lightning, and whether or not they manage to hold water . . . or electricity.

GET DOWN

For years, experts would tell people to lie or crouch down if they found themselves caught out in an open field during a thunderstorm. The rationale, they said, was to make yourself the lowest object in the area, since lightning always goes for the tallest object around.

FALSE Lightning will strike the ground pretty frequently, and you can't get lower than the ground without digging yourself into a hole. The safest place to be during a thunderstorm is inside a sturdy structure—crouching down is tantamount to just giving up and hoping you don't get zapped.

DON'T SHOWER

Your mom always told you it was a bad idea to take a shower during a thunderstorm. She was right about a few other things over the years— was this one of them?

TRUE Even if you reside in a modern house, lightning can easily travel through a building's plumbing system, even if the pipes are made of polyvinyl chloride (PVC). Water is an excellent conductor of electricity, and if lightning should strike outside of your building, the electricity can snake its way into your water pipes and travel through the plumbing into your home. Smelling clean and feeling fresh aren't worth the jolt.

UNPLUG YOURSELF

Old movies often show people frantically unplugging appliances before a storm hits. Was this just a crazy idea?

TRUE Lightning can also travel through the electrical system in your house, shorting out your appliances and gadgets, and also potentially giving you a nasty shock if you're using the wrong device at the wrong time. Unplugging everything is mostly unnecessary these days, but it's a good idea to unplug your computer and stay off of landline telephones while an electrical storm is in the area. Use surge protectors for expensive electronics.

DOUBLE JEOPARDY

We've heard a million times that "lightning doesn't strike twice." What's the scoop?

FALSE Lightning can strike the same spot a hundred times—it's just one of those things we tell ourselves to feel better about our odds of turning into fried bologna. There are videos on the Internet that show lightning striking the same spire on a skyscraper dozens of times in the span of a few minutes. Just because lightning struck your backyard once doesn't mean you're free to go back out there. Never test your luck against the an angry atmosphere.

CONTACT HIGH

There's an old, persistent story that people who are struck by lightning are still electrified, so you have to avoid touching them at all costs if you don't want to get zapped yourself.

FALSE Lightning victims will need immediate medical attention, especially if the jolt stopped their heart. Odds are they can still be revived, so falling for some strange lie that they're electrified means that you're letting someone die for absolutely no reason at all. Help the poor person, for crying out loud!

REMAIN INDOORS

For something that can kill you faster than the blink of an eye, lightning sure is one of nature's most beautiful displays. And it's safe for you to watch it from the window, since glass doesn't conduct electricity. Right?

FALSE While it's highly unlikely that you'll suffer a direct lightning strike through a closed, sealed window, the heat and shockwave can certainly shatter the glass, injuring you and anyone nearby. Enjoy the light show from a safe distance indoors.

PREPARE FOR A THUNDERSTORM

A nice rainfall can be refreshing, but it can quickly turn deadly. Thunderstorms may be somewhat small compared to hurricanes, but they still carry significant destructive force and average 15 miles in diameter.

All thunderstorms are dangerous, as they produce deadly lightning and often high winds and hail. There are approximately 100,000 thunderstorms each year in the U.S., roughly 10 percent of which are classified as "severe" by the National Weather Service—meaning they boast damaging winds of at least 58 MPH or hail at least 1 inch in diameter.

To be safe, you should always seek shelter before a thunderstorm hits—so if you do hear the rumbling, go indoors. Fully enclosed buildings offer the best protection. Their electrical wiring and metal piping can offer a grounding effect in the event of a lightning strike. And of course, the building itself will provide shelter from all the wind and blowing debris. During the storm, just stay away from conductive things like wiring, corded telephones, and plumbing pipes and fixtures. Continue to avoid these items for 30 minutes after the storm, in case of lingering lightning.

129 TREE-PROOF YOUR HOME

Large, mature trees can help increase the value of your property—unless they crash into your house after a major storm. If you live somewhere frequently hit by windy storms, it's likely to happen eventually. Prune weak, damaged, or dead limbs, and ask your local power company if they have a program for pruning.

CULL THE HERD The best way to tree-proof your home is to remove all trees from your yard that could reach your house if they were to fall.

PLANT DEFENSIVELY Saplings planted today will eventually grow up to become trees that might pose a danger to your house. Pick spots where the trees won't threaten your home, your neighbor's house, or external features like power lines and propane tanks. Don't plant brittle species that break easily, such as elm, willow, box elder, poplar, and silver maple. Where ice storms are a possibility, don't plant trees that hold their leaves late into the fall. The weight of ice on leaves can bring down limbs or entire trees.

ASK NICELY If the tree that's looming over your house should belong to your neighbors, use diplomacy to get them to remove it. That task will be easier if you can convince them that the tree is a danger to their house too.

WEATHER WORLD RECORDS
HEAVIEST RAINFALL

It's pretty easy for there to be phenomenal amounts of rain from a thunderstorm during the wet season, but not many of these storms have approached levels seen in the heaviest storms ever observed. Unionville, Maryland, saw 1.23 inches of rain in just one minute on July 4, 1956, while Holt, Missouri, floated into the record books when it saw one foot of rain in one hour on June 22, 1947.

130 DEAL WITH A DOWNED TREE

When severe weather hits, downed trees follow. Make like a lumberjack and use the proper technique to cut up a tree on the ground—a process called bucking.

STEP 1 Remove all major branches, then brace the underside of the tree with wood to keep it stable and off the ground.

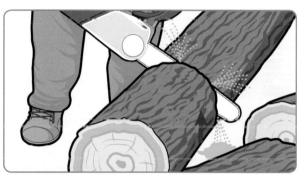

STEP 2 Standing uphill from the tree, start by cutting the underside of the trunk about one-third of the way through with a chainsaw. Then come back to the top side and finish the cut so it runs all the way through the trunk.

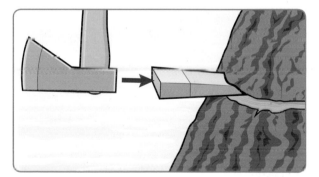

STEP 3 Gravity should pull that trunk section off the tree, but if your saw gets stuck in the cut, shut it off right away. Drive a wedge into the cut to loosen the tension, and then remove the saw.

131 MINIMIZE WIND DAMAGE TO YOUR HOME

How can wind damage a home? The most common form of damage is largely superficial, when gusty winds blow away roofing materials like shingles or tiles, tear off vinyl siding, or cause screens, gutters, and any other decorative items to come loose and fly away in the torrent of air. More serious damage can occur when winds exceed hurricane force, and airborne debris shatters windows, damages walls, or even weakens and eventually tears away the entire roof. Poorly constructed buildings and those made from lightweight materials (like mobile or prefab homes) can be completely destroyed by very strong straight-line winds. This diagram shows you how you can protect your home. If you're unsure how to check these things, it's worth it to have a home inspector give your house a once-over. Your insurance company may offer this service or be able to recommend a good resource.

Check roof sheathing is securely nailed down.

Ensure shingles are firmly nailed down and well fitted.

Cover all windows, sliding-glass doors, French doors, and skylights with storm shutters to prevent broken glass.

Do not drain or cover your pool.

Garage doors should be properly braced (see item 88).

Be sure lawn furniture, toys, garbage bins, and other items that might become projectiles in a high wind are securely stowed before a storm, or battened down.

Be sure the connection between roof and walls is tight enough to keep updrafts from lifting off the roof.

Make sure siding and shutters are firmly attached.

Ensure HVAC units, skylights, and pipes are tightly affixed.

Triple-hinged doors will be much safer than double-hinged.

All external doors should have a deadbolt.

Be sure all cracks are well sealed. This keeps you warm and saves energy, but also ensures wind doesn't cause interior damage.

Any tree that might threaten your home should be safely pruned or, worst case, removed entirely.

132 WATCH OUT FOR MICROBURSTS

The most common type of damaging wind you'll encounter during a thunderstorm is a downburst, which is just about as ominous as the name suggests. Every thunderstorm contains a downdraft, which acts just like a car's exhaust pipe, allowing dense, rain-cooled air to flow out of the base of the storm and away as a gust front or an outflow boundary. When one of these outflow boundaries reaches your location, you feel a noticeable drop in temperature followed by gusty winds. If you're in a plane, these can be very dangerous, but pilots are well trained to avoid them.

Downbursts can impact the ground at speeds of more than 100 MPH. You're probably most familiar with the term "microburst," which is a downburst that occurs on a small scale, sometimes affecting an area just the size of a few city blocks. There are several types of microbursts, of course, because nothing can be simple.

DRY MICROBURSTS These are most common in drier climates where there's less moisture for thunderstorms to work with. Thunderstorms in these high and dry areas can form with layers of dry air beneath them, causing rain to evaporate before it can reach the ground. This evaporation causes the air to cool and become denser than its surroundings, forcing it to sink toward the ground. The air sinks faster as it speeds toward the ground, ultimately impacting the surface with powerful winds.

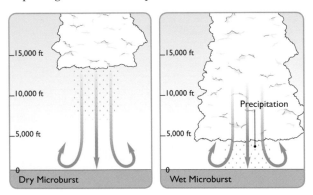

Dry Microburst

Wet Microburst

WET MICROBURSTS These result from two rather nerdily named processes: "dry air entrainment" and "water loading." Dry air entrainment refers to dry air mixing into a thunderstorm at the mid levels, causing some rain to evaporate, creating dense, rain-cooled air that falls toward the surface. Water loading, or the incredibly heavy weight of the storm's water, can help drag this bubble of dense air toward the ground even faster, and it slams the surface with some hefty force. From a distance, a wet microburst looks like a huge, gray water balloon careening toward the ground from the base of a thunderstorm.

133 BRACE FOR DEADLY WINDS

When you can look up at the sky from your living room and wonder where your roof went, it feels like splitting hairs to try to figure out the pattern of the winds that blew the cap off your house. Damaging winds are damaging winds, after all, but they can come from very different beasts, and you should probably know what you'll be facing in your area.

STRAIGHT-LINE WINDS	TORNADIC WINDS
HOW THEY MOVE As you might guess, in a straight line. The strongest straight-line winds can exceed hurricane force.	**HOW THEY MOVE** Spin around in a circular fashion.
DAMAGE Usually cause damage to trees, power lines, loose objects, and vulnerable structures like old barns or poorly constructed backyard forts and sheds.	**DAMAGE** Can cause more damage than straight-line winds; debris gets more opportunities to destroy other objects, creating more flying debris, and so on.
SIGNS Blow everything in the same direction like a giant, airy steamroller.	**SIGNS** Deposit debris in a circular pattern—sometimes even creating cycloidal markings, or swirling scars, in the earth itself.

WEATHER WORLD RECORDS
THE MAN WHO ANGERED THOR

The odds that any one object will get struck by lightning are pretty low, and the odds that any single person will be hit are even lower. That's why it's astounding that Roy Sullivan, a park ranger in West Virginia, was struck not once, but seven times during a 35-year period between the 1940s and 1970s.

134 DRIVE IN HIGH WINDS

When you discount the threats of flying debris and falling trees, strong winds are less of a hazard inside vehicles than they are outside, but crosswinds can still make it very hard (if not impossible) to control your vehicle. You'll also have to contend with the fact that visibility will be very low—if not zero—along with the possibility that high-profile vehicles like box trucks or 18-wheelers will tip over under the enormous force of strong winds. Here are some basic tips if you can't get off the road and the winds are rising.

STAY AWAY FROM TRAILERS Whether we're talking about those 18-wheelers, or boats on trailers, or a basic U-Haul, the fact is the driver has very little control over what happens to that trailer in a high wind, and the whole thing probably has high non-aerodynamic profile. Stay back.

SLOW DOWN It's tempting to want to get off the highway as quickly as possible—and maybe even a little exhilarating if the wind's behind you. But your ability to correct when that same wind shifts its direction and pushes you off course is somewhat limited. High wind reduces friction. It causes your car to lift a bit, it shoves the car off its line, and it's often accompanied by rain. None of this is good for your control of the vehicle.

WATCH FOR DEBRIS Tree limbs may be blown onto the road, soil embankments may slide into your lane, and that idiot ahead who hasn't tied his mattress down is really regretting that decision. Another reason to take it slow.

135 DRIVE SAFELY IN HEAVY RAIN

While driving in the rain won't be as white-knuckle terrifying as being on the road while in a blizzard or hailstorm, it's not exactly safe or fun either, with the slippery streets and low visibility. Below are a few things to keep in mind. But remember, if the rain is coming down so hard that you can't see, the safest thing to do is to pull as far off the road as possible and wait for it to pass. Turn on your hazard lights so that you're not hit by someone trying to do the same thing!

SLOW DOWN Yes, it's obvious. It's also important. Even great drivers can still end up in crashes due to slippery roads, low visibility, and all those other drivers who aren't as awesome as you. It's a good rule of thumb to keep more than three seconds of distance between you and the car you're following in bad weather. So ride those brakes with pride.

DON'T PUDDLE JUMP Never drive straight through a large puddle unless you're 100% sure how deep it is (like, you just saw another car drive through it). It might be concealing a car-killer of a pothole, or be deep enough that the water could damage your electrical system.

DOUBLE TAP That said, when you do go driving through a big puddle, tap your brake pedal lightly to help dry your rotors.

DON'T GET SWEPT AWAY Never try to drive through running water. Every year, places with heavy rainfall have stories of cars getting stuck or even swept away when trying to cross seemingly insignificant water obstacles.

136 COPE WITH A POWER LINE

You really shouldn't be out driving in a major storm. You do know that, right? But sometimes it happens. And sometimes the truly unexpected and terrifying happens. That's the case for those unlucky few folks who have happened to be driving by right as the wind took out a nearby power pole. If a power line falls on your car and disables it while you're inside, you'll have to take action. But what on Earth to do?

PUT OUT AN S.O.S. The safest thing to do is to remain in your vehicle and phone for help.

JUMP FREE If you absolutely must leave the vehicle because of fire or some other danger, avoid touching any portion of your car's metal frame. The greatest peril will come from touching the car and the ground at the same time, since the electricity could travel through you into the ground, causing injury or death. Jump as far away from the car as you can, landing with your feet together.

SHUFFLE OFF TO SAFETY Keep both feet in contact with each other and the ground as you move away. Avoid pools of water, which conduct electricity.

137 STOP HYDROPLANING

When tires encounter more water than the tread grooves can dissipate, the tire essentially floats on a layer of water. That's hydroplaning—and it ain't good.

READ THE CLUES When hydroplaning, the engine's revolutions per minute (RPM) will sharply increase, and the wheels will have no traction.

EASE UP Don't turn the wheel or hit the brakes, since either will cause a skid. Instead, hold your course and ease off the accelerator, allowing your vehicle to slow down and the tires to penetrate the water layer.

138 DRIVE SAFELY ON FLOODED ROADS

Every year, people lose their lives when their vehicles get washed away as they try to drive on flooded roads.

STUDY THE NUMBERS A simple 6 inches of water will cause most cars to lose control and possibly stall. Double that amount, and most cars just give up and float. At 2 feet of rushing water, vehicles are at risk of being swept away (even trucks and four-wheel drives). If floodwaters are starting to swirl around your vehicle, abandon it—and save your life.

DON'T HEAD INTO THE UNKNOWN Beneath the water, pavement might be ripped away, leaving a hole that could swallow your vehicle. The rule for driving through water is simple: If you can't see the road surface or its line markings, take a detour. As the saying goes, "Turn around, don't drown."

140
FIGHT BACK AGAINST FLOODING

Staying safe during a flood takes a combination of proper planning and quick thinking. Always be aware of flood hazards, especially if you're in a low-lying area, near a river or bay, or downstream from a dam. In low-lying or flood-prone areas, a NOAA (National Oceanic and Atmospheric Administration) weather radio with an alarm can be a lifesaving investment.

BE READY If you have a day or more to prepare, move important things to the highest and driest location in your home. Pack any and all important and irreplaceable papers, photos, files, and data to take with you if you evacuate.

BE AWARE Stay very alert to flood watches and warnings for your local area and the areas upriver and upland from your location.

MOVE FAST If you only have minutes to get out, don't waste time gathering possessions. Things can be replaced, but lives cannot. Don't wait to be told to move to higher ground if authorities say flash flooding is possible.

STOCK WATER Contamination can be a big deal during and after a flood, so make sure you have a safe supply of a gallon of water per person per day (don't forget pets!)—both in your home and if you evacuate.

BUG OUT RIGHT Be prepared to evacuate far in advance, and be sure that your car is also stocked with plenty of cash, no-cook foods, spare clothes, sanitation items, your cell-phone charger, rain gear, and other essential supplies in the event you have to provide for yourself and your family for some time.

DON'T DIG IN Never decide that you're smarter than the experts and that you can ride out the storm. If you are told to evacuate: DO IT! And as you go, beware of streams, ditches, drainage channels, canyons, and other low-lying regions. Flash floods can happen in these places even far away from the rainstorms.

DRIVE SAFELY Never drive through even the shallowest floodwaters—turn around and find another path. Even seemingly safe water can pick up your car and sweep it away.

139
SAFELY CROSS A RIVER

Remember geometry from grade school? Good, because basic knowledge of triangles can keep you from getting sucked into a fast-moving river. If the one who's braving the current is backed up by two friends on shore—with a sturdy rope loop connecting all three—the two on land will be able to help the one in the water, even if he or she loses footing. Once the first person has reached the far bank, the second can cross, using the rope stretched between the banks as a safety line. When the last person is ready to cross, he or she enters the water, and the others pull him or her across.

141 FIND THE FLOODPLAINS

Flooding isn't exactly a surprise along the banks of a waterway, especially in areas known as floodplains. A floodplain is the land on either side of a river or stream that is prone to flooding when the body of water swells over its banks. Even though we know that floodplains flood (I mean, it is in the name, after all), humans have for thousands of years built settlements along these susceptible stretches of waterlogged land.

Hundreds of millions of people live in cities situated along the floodplains of major rivers such as the Congo, Yangtze, Mississippi, and Amazon. These plains are vital in the development of both world history (think of the Fertile Crescent) and the agriculture that sustains us today. We build cities along rivers not only for the fertile land, but also because rivers are major transportation routes that can link small, inland towns to the rest of the world. However, these benefits are tempered with an obvious downside: One major flood carries the ability to wipe out an entire town, threatening the lives of thousands (if not millions) of people.

Some floodplains are easily visible on satellite images, even when the water level is normal, as the extent of the fertile soil on either side of a river usually gives away the locations that flood most often. The area typically known as the Mississippi River Delta is one of the most famous floodplains in the English-speaking world, and it's visible from above as a low-lying area of lush, fertile land along the river's banks from Missouri through Louisiana.

EXTREME WEATHER HISTORY:
CHINA'S GREAT FLOOD OF 1931

When we think about droughts, we usually focus on the protracted periods without rain. But in 1931 in Central China, the residents discovered that the end of a drought isn't always a welcome sight. After two years of dry weather, a confluence of environmental factors combined to cause one of the single deadliest events of the 20th century. The exact death toll will likely never be known, but at least 145,000 people were killed. Some estimates put that number ten times higher, with Western sources estimating an actual death toll between 3.75 and 4 million people. The flood impacted a population of nearly 30 million people.

The catastrophic flooding began on the heels of a severe drought. The cycle broke in the form of heavy snowfalls, which then melted in spring to flood the Yangtze and Huai rivers. In addition to all of the winter runoff, the spring and summer rainstorms brought unusually heavy rainfall. Four weather stations along the Yangtze measured 2 feet of rain in July alone.

The flood's high death toll was due to a combination of rising waters and poor geography. The waters quickly reached the city of Nanjing, China's capital at the time. The city was in the middle of a massive floodplain, and the flood overwhelmed dykes and levees, with a high water mark 53 feet above the flood level. On August 25, 1931, floodwaters rushed through the Grand Canal, drowning approximately 200,000 people in the their sleep. Those who did survive the initial flooding were subjected to diseases such as typhus and cholera. Horrific stories emerged of victims even resorting to infanticide and cannibalism to survive.

Many of contemporary China's flood-control measures, like the Three Gorges Dam project, were begun in direct response to the catastrophe.

142 LIVE THROUGH A FLASH FLOOD

You're exploring a canyon when, all of a sudden, the air rumbles like a subwoofer. Then you see it: a wall of water churning with felled trees and boulders. And it's headed your way.

KNOW THE AREA You can avoid this hair-raising situation by staying away from flood-prone zones that are in the path of natural drainage areas like riverbeds or canyons. If you're on the coast, beware of storm surges during tropical storms and hurricanes.

HIGHTAIL IT TO HIGH GROUND To escape a flash flood, leave everything behind and then run for high ground as fast as you can. If the water starts to rise around you, climb a tree or scramble onto a large rock—anything that will get you higher.

RIDE IT OUT If you end up in the flow, keep your head and upper body safe at all costs. Point your feet downstream and try to deflect—or better yet, steer clear of—obstructions like rocks and trees.

GET A GRIP You won't be able to fight the current, but you may be able to gradually work your way toward the edge of the flood so you can catch hold of a tree or bush and pull yourself out of the water.

HOLE UP AT HOME If a flash flood hits your home, arm yourself with the essentials, including food, water, a battery-operated radio, matches, and candles, and then head to the upper floors. Unless your home's foundation is threatened and on the verge of collapse, stay put until the waters recede.

DENNIS DEBUNKS:
FLOODING . . . IT CAN'T HAPPEN HERE!

You get a flash flood warning. "I'll be okay," you think, "we're not in a flood zone." Unfortunately, places that don't typically flood when rivers and creeks rise can flood when water overwhelms storm sewers. Flash flooding can inundate buildings and roads that typically don't flood during less intense situations, so it's wise to pay attention and get ready to take action if heavy storms threaten.

143 PADDLE THROUGH FLOODWATERS

A canoe can be a great way for you to navigate or escape from floodwaters. But there's a huge difference between fighting your way out of a hazard-filled flood zone and paddling down a lazy river.

SIT FOR STABILITY Place yourself slightly behind the middle of the boat with your weight low and centered.

TRY TO STAY DRY You know that floodwater is full of nasty stuff, so do your very best to stay out of it. No trailing your fingers in the water on this trip!

AVOID HIDDEN OBSTACLES Avoid any swirls on the water's surface, since they may indicate a submerged object. In a big flood, you might encounter overfalls, areas where water crosses a highway or other submerged feature. Overfalls often hide whirlpools and rapids, so steer away from them if you can.

PADDLE AWAY To steer a canoe through the current as straight as possible, stroke powerfully on alternating sides. Or use a strong J-stroke, while turning and pushing the blade slightly outward at the end of the stroke to better control your speed and course.

144 RESCUE SOMEONE CAUGHT IN A FLOOD

The fast current of a flash flood is one of its biggest dangers. But if someone is trapped by a flash flood—clinging to a tree branch or perched on the roof of a car—try using that speed to your advantage.

STEP 1 Coil a rescue rope and throw it upstream of the person you're rescuing, allowing the current to carry the line to the victim. Instruct that person to tie the rope around his or her waist.

STEP 2 Tie the rescue rope around a tree or another solid object to anchor it against the weight of the victim and the flowing water's immense pressure.

STEP 3 Once secured to the rope, the victim can leave his or her perch and work toward the shore.

145 BE AWARE OF HOME SAFETY

Flooding can do a lot more than simply sweeping away homes and vehicles like they were twigs in front of a garden hose. Residents cleaning up from floods can run into economic losses, mold, chemicals, and even some unfriendly visitors. When the waters finally recede and you're really tired of living in motels (or, worst case scenario, relief camps), it's really tempting to just get back

home as soon as possible, put on some rubber gloves and a can-do smile, and start cleaning up. But your health is more important than getting things tidied up, so do be aware of what could go wrong.

CONTAMINATION Floodwaters are disgusting—they can carry hazardous materials like human and animal waste, toxic chemicals, oil, and gasoline, not to mention the bodies of anything (or anyone) who drowned—and all of this water seeps into anything it touches. Many homes are condemned by flooding after a hurricane simply because of contamination from the toxic slurry, as well as the thick layers of mold the moisture leaves behind once the water recedes. Don't drink the water until it's been tested and cleared.

HOME INVASION Those who are lucky enough to have homes to return to once the waters recede can find some ugly surprises on the walls. Mold is a huge and costly issue that plagues buildings after a flood; the mold is even worse if the water was especially deep or the flood occurred during the warmer months. The mold can be so thick and toxic that some homes are torn down because the task of removing it is too costly (or just downright dangerous). In addition, don't forget about all of the snakes, spiders, ants, and any other unfriendly creatures that are displaced. They can cling to any floating debris, providing an unwelcome surprise if you have to go wading.

EXTREME WEATHER AROUND THE WORLD: THE NETHERLANDS

It can be hard to prevent and control flooding under the best of circumstances, but what if the ocean is actually champing at the bit to reclaim your country? More than half of the Netherlands, nestled along the banks of the North Sea, lies around sea level, with just a little over a quarter of the country actually positioned below sea level. When you're sitting below an entire sea full of water, gravity tends to win out more often than not.

Flooding is one of the greatest threats to life in the Netherlands, and its residents have struggled against the tug and pull of its neighboring sea for as long as humans have populated the strip of land on which the country sits. The natural solution to the problem is to put a wall between dry land and the water next door, and that's exactly what they did.

The Netherlands are protected by a system of dikes (also called levees, or earthen walls) and floodgates that help control floodwaters and keep water from reclaiming the land. This protection system has mostly been successful in recent years—the country hasn't seen a major flood disaster since the middle of the 1900s.

146 DON'T GET CAUGHT IN A SLIDE

Mudslides occur when sloping ground becomes so saturated with water that the soil loses its grip and gravity takes over. Then you get to deal with a filthy deluge that can destroy your property and put your life at risk. Be smart and heed these warning signs:

KNOW THE STORY Mudslides are recurring events that happen where they've happened before. Contact local authorities to learn the geographical history of your area, including any fires that have destroyed vegetation (which can often lead to soil erosion) or construction that has altered water flow.

AVOID EXTREME INCLINES Steep slopes that are close to the edge of a mountain range or valley are bad news. If you can, simply live somewhere else that's less vulnerable.

WATCH THE WATER Pay attention to changes in the patterns of storm-water drainage on slopes. If there's a river or stream nearby, sudden changes in water level—or a change in color from clear to brown—could indicate an impending slide.

MIND THE GAPS Cracks in pavement, or walls pulling away from buildings, indicate that the land is moving—which means that it may be vulnerable to mudslides. This is also true if cracks appear in your house's foundation, or if doors and windows start to stick in their frames.

LOOK FOR CROOKED STUFF Any trees or telephone poles that are starting to lean are not charming quirks. They mean the soil is eroding, and you should watch out.

RIO
CATARATAS

147 RIDE OUT A MUDSLIDE

Mudslides can be spawned by a wide variety of things: heavy storms, earthquakes, volcanic eruptions, or just plain old erosion. However they get their start, they're pretty much always a dirty bad time. Your best survival strategy is to shore up your home against slides before it's too late. Failing that, here are some survival hints.

STAY AWAKE Most mudslide-related deaths occur at night, when people are asleep. If the rain is coming down hard and flooding and slides are predicted, put on a pot of coffee and continue to monitor weather and evacuation reports.

LISTEN FOR THE RUMBLE Massive amounts of soil, water, and debris don't just come down silently. If you hear a rumbling sound emanating from uphill, evacuate immediately.

GET OUT OF THE SLIDE'S PATH Sometimes, there won't be time to evacuate. If you get caught in a mudslide, the best you can do is try to move out of its way. If it's too late for that, curl up into a tight ball and fold your arms over your head for protection.

148 DIG YOUR TRUCK OUT OF THE MUD

Getting your vehicle stuck in the mud can ruin your day. But when you're in a major flood and your escape-mobile starts spinning its wheels, this annoyance can escalate to a possibly deadly situation. Here's how to free your ride:

TAKE YOUR FOOT OFF THE GAS You don't want to dig deeper ruts and toss around the remaining solid ground under the wheels, so quit stomping the gas.

GO BACK AND FORTH Put the car in reverse, then switch gears and drive forward; the wheels may pick up enough traction to move. Try it a few times.

KICK OUT YOUR PASSENGERS Have anyone in the car get out while you drive forward.

DIG A DITCH Using whatever tool you have on hand, hollow out a hole in the mud just ahead of each tire. Give each hole a slightly upward slope, then drive forward very gently and, with any luck, up the incline.

IMPROVISE GRIP Search your vehicle along with the surrounding environment for things such as branches, wood planks, or blankets, and then lay them immediately in front of the wheels. Then gently drive the vehicle over these objects onto firmer ground.

WEATHER WORLD RECORDS
LARGEST MUDSLIDE

Mudslides are a regular threat to the millions of people who live in hilly and mountainous regions around the world, but rainfall isn't the only thing that can turn mountainsides into a deadly torrent of mud and debris. The catastrophic eruption of Mount St. Helens in Washington in 1980 also triggered the largest mudslide ever recorded. The scalding ejecta caused billions of tons of soil to roar into Spirit Lake, doubling the lake's size and raising its elevation by 100 feet.

Just as you can't let your guard down when a flash flood warning goes up, you shouldn't let your guard down after a particularly rainy stretch of weather if you live near hills or mountains. Mud- and landslides can happen in unlikely places and often occur without warning. However, certain places are more prone to slides than others—the devastating mudslide that killed more than 40 people in Oso, Washington, in March 2014 came after decades of studies and warnings by scientists.

149 PROTECT YOUR HOME

To prevent your dream home from turning into a muddy nightmare, take these steps.

STEP 1 If you suspect your house may be in a slide zone, have a geological assessment done. Better yet, do that before you buy the home.

STEP 2 Think about the drainage on your property. If your home or yard often floods, use gravity to direct the flow of water away from your foundation. Dig a trench 1 to 2 feet deep and equally wide, and line it with compacted limestone.

STEP 3 Build a vertical retaining wall, which acts as a buffer and prevents land from sliding all the way down a hillside, taking your home with it. A good rule of thumb is to build a system of walls no more than 2 feet in height, staggered down the hillside. Be sure to provide drainage behind the walls, otherwise the soil will erode and then destabilize them.

STEP 4 Topsoil needs some strongly rooted vegetation to keep it in place. Start out with a solid carpeting of sod, followed by trees and a few faster-growing shrubs such as privets or decorative perennials such as roses.

EXTREME WEATHER HISTORY:
VARGAS, VENEZUELA

It's easy to prepare for the disasters we know could happen, but it is virtually impossible to prepare for a tragedy thought impossible until it unfolds. One of the worst weather disasters in recent history occurred along the northern coast of Venezuela in December 1999, during an unprecedented storm in the region.

The rugged, mountainous coast of the state of Vargas in northern Venezuela is a slice of paradise from an environmental standpoint, with luscious green hills stretching for miles along the gorgeous coastline of the Caribbean Sea. Residents were little prepared for the storms that cropped up in the middle of December 1999, which dropped a mind-boggling 3 feet of rain over the course of three days, overwhelming the land's ability to absorb the water.

This enormous influx of rainwater weakened the soil to its breaking point, triggering devastating mud- and landslides up and down the entire coast in Vargas. Whole towns were swept into the sea—buildings and residents alike—when the ground gave way. The death toll climbed into the tens of thousands by the time that the ground finally stabilized and the disaster was over.

150 BUILD A FIRE IN THE RAIN

Fire and water? Really? Yes, it can be done. Here's how.

DON'T RUSH Allow three times as much time for fire-building as you'd need in dry conditions. If you're hiking, gather dry tinder as you go along the trail.

LOOK DOWN Dry tinder may be under rocks, ledges, and logs, and in tree hollows. The underside of leaning deadfalls can be dry in a downpour; chop out chunks of good wood. Conifer stumps hold flammable resins.

LOOK UP Search for dry kindling and fuel off the wet ground. Fallen branches that are suspended in smaller trees will likely be rot-free. Locate a dense conifer and harvest the low, dead twigs and branches that die off as the tree grows. Shred the bark with your fingers.

SCRAPE BY Use a knife or hatchet blade to scrape away wet surfaces from wood before adding it to the fire.

Once the fire's going strong, construct a crosshatched "log cabin" of wet wood around it with a double-layered roof. The top layer of wood will deflect rain while the lower level dries.

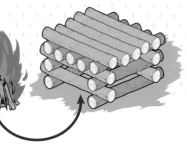

151 CHOOSE YOUR CAMPGROUND WISELY

It sounds simple enough, but many campers fail to take basic precautions against flooding. After all, on our list of things that scare us, flash floods don't seem as terrifying as a tornado or wildfire. However, flash floods do pose a particular danger to campers. If you have set up a tent in the wilderness, chances are you've camped out in the rain. But heavy rainfall in the wrong place can create a deadly situation. In 2010, a popular Arkansas campground saw the Little Missouri River rise from 3 feet to 23 feet overnight, and 20 people perished in the deluge. Here are some precautions to help you stay not only dry, but alive.

TAKE THE HIGH GROUND It can be tempting to camp on terrain that is flat, or even protected by natural earthen walls, but you just might be camping in low-lying terrain prone to flooding. Pay attention to terrain. Water usually follows a predictable path, so avoid any gullies and washouts that, in the event of heavy rainfall, will fill up first with rushing water.

KNOW THE AREA You should always have a battery-powered radio, but it won't do you that much good if you're not familiar with the names of surrounding towns and counties. These areas will be referenced in any warnings, and knowing your location relative to any weather alerts will help you stay prepared.

GAS UP Keep your vehicle's gas tank full in case you need to evacuate. It's also a good idea to park your vehicle facing the exit. The last thing you want to do is have to execute a three-point turn on water-soaked land or in thickening mud.

LISTEN Especially in areas prone to flooding, you will often be able to hear the oncoming water from a fast-filling gully or wash-out. It might be sunny where you are, but an upstream thunderstorm can drop enough water to flood your area.

PLAN IT OUT Always have an evacuation plan. If you're hiking in low-lying terrain, take a moment to find the high ground, and know the fastest and easiest way to get there.

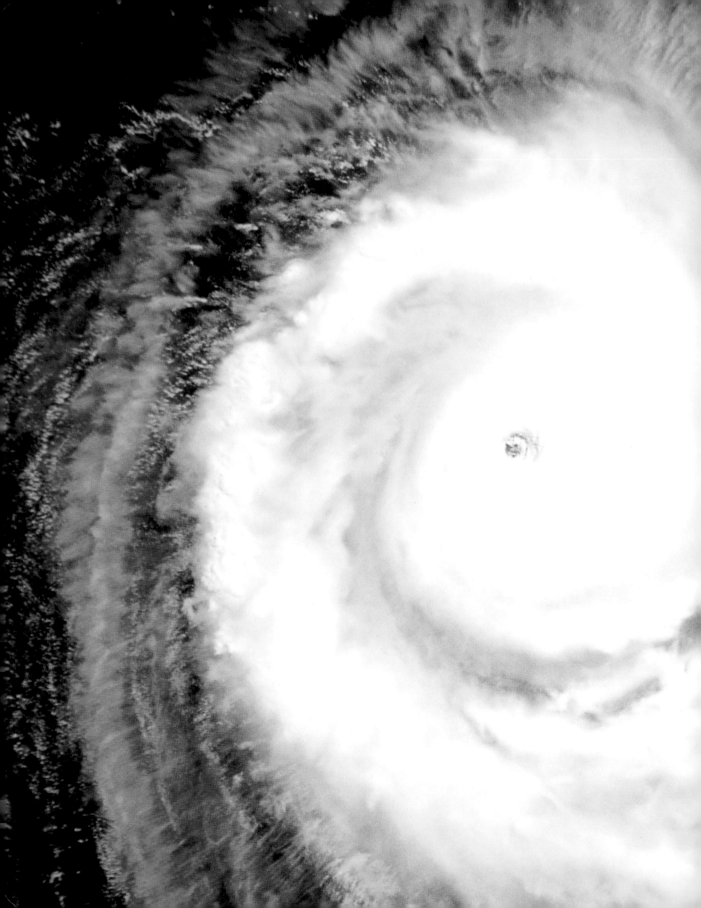

Welcome to summer, a season that all too often invokes the same set of feelings as spilling a freshly opened soda on your lap: anger, discomfort, stickiness, despair, and acceptance. Summer sneaks up on you like boiling water on a frog (seriously, who first thought to do that?)—you carelessly enjoy the mild spring weather until you realize you can't go outside without longing for a cold bottle of water. It's uncomfortable. But though it's hard for most of us to truly enjoy the weather, it's something we get used to along the way.

During this three month period of the year, our hemisphere stares the sun right in the face—though, contrary to popular belief, we're not actually closer to the sun during the summer than we are during the winter. Our hemisphere is just tilted differently, allowing the sun's direct rays to beat down into the atmosphere and roast us during the intense daylight hours. The sun climbs higher above the horizon, the days get longer, the bugs get louder, and the air gets thicker.

Perhaps the best thing about summer is the stormy weather that accompanies its arrival. The one true upside to a brutally disgusting afternoon in July is the inevitable thunderstorm that brings a burst of temperate air and douses the town in a torrent of cool water. Ahhh, that's the stuff. The heat of the summer also allows nature to throw temper tantrums, unleashing spectacular displays of lightning around the hemisphere, swirling up the biggest hurricanes, and letting loose photogenic squall lines that run across the countryside with a ferocity that shakes even the weather-hardiest among us.

Summer is aggressive, oppressive, and thrilling. It takes a keen mind to recognize the season's dangers, and to act quickly to ensure survival in the face of nature's most organized tumult. The following chapter will help you survive and thrive in even the most unbearable summers you'll encounter on your many trips around the sun.

152 BEWARE OF CYCLONES

Owning a home on a pristine beach in a tropical paradise is a dream come true for a lucky few people. Living just a few feet away from everlasting warmth, brilliant sunshine, rolling waves, and sandy shores is a cozy thought that keeps many of us working hard, hoping for that big break (or the right lottery numbers). One of the downsides to living along the coast in a warm part of the world, though, is a threat that reliably lurks offshore several times a year—tropical cyclones.

A tropical cyclone is a highly organized center of low pressure over the ocean that can feature destructive winds, torrential rainfall, devastating storm surges, and often tornadoes. Nature's way of balancing the atmosphere's temperature, these storms form in the tropics and race toward the poles in an ultimately futile attempt to redistribute heat and achieve thermal harmony.

Tropical cyclones have different names around the world. Those of us who live in North America and Europe know these storms as "hurricanes," while those tropical cyclones that develop in the western Pacific Ocean are called "typhoons." In the Southern Hemisphere and Indian Ocean, these systems are simply "cyclones." Throughout the rest of this chapter, we'll interchangeably use the terms "hurricane" and "tropical cyclone."

To further confuse things, these terms—hurricane, typhoon, and cyclone—all refer to the storm when it's at its strongest stage. What are the other stages? Glad you asked. Around North America, we have four levels of tropical cyclone development, all based on the strength of the storm's winds at the surface.

TROPICAL DEPRESSION
A weak tropical cyclone is beginning to develop.
38 MPH or lower

TROPICAL STORM
The storm gains strength and becomes more organized.
Between 39 and 73 MPH

HURRICANE
The storm continues to grow in strength and focus.
74 MPH or stronger

MAJOR HURRICANE
Rare, intense hurricanes that can level an entire city.
111 MPH or stronger

153 RATE YOUR HOME'S SAFETY

How likely is your home to survive a major hurricane? The answer depends on a wide range of variables (how bad is the storm? What's its exact path? Where did it make landfall?), but here are some basic points to consider.

HOME'S AGE In 2002, many areas upgraded their hurricane codes; homes built after that have an advantage.

ROOFING MATERIALS Is your roof made of shingles or tiles? Older shingles can blow off in storms and cracked tiles can cause damage to the entire roof if the wind gets underneath them. Climb up there before storm season starts and make repairs as needed (even one or two bad tiles can lead to trouble).

CONSTRUCTION Gabled roofs are a bit less secure; you're safer if you have a "hip roof." A hip roof is closed on all sides, versus a gabled roof, which has an open triangle, making it more likely to catch the wind. You'll also want hurricane shutters.

DEBRIS What surrounds your home? You already know that you need to stash lawn furniture, bikes, and such before a storm (you know that, right?), but are there items you don't have control over that could blow into your home and damage it?

EXTREME WEATHER AROUND THE WORLD:
PACIFIC CYCLONES

The waters off the coast of western Mexico are extremely warm, which fosters quite the rambunctious hurricane season most years. Storms generally form from tropical waves that bubble up near the coast, slowly organizing into formidable cyclones as they move west or northwest away from land. But if the steering currents are blowing in the wrong direction, these storms will hook back toward land, creating life-threatening conditions for the millions of people who live along Mexico's coasts.

The western Pacific Ocean can see 30 or more typhoons or tropical storms develop every year, threatening hundreds of millions of people with every swipe close to land. Japan and the Philippines are at greatest risk from typhoons, but every country in the region north of the equator is at risk each year. By contrast, the southeastern Pacific Ocean is far too cold (and the air far too stable) for cyclones to form.

154 BE READY TO GO

There may not be a lot of good things to say about hurricanes, but at least they generally give some warning that they're coming. Of course, sometimes the Next Great Storm fizzles out over the ocean, or one that's predicted to be relatively mild picks up steam and causes unexpected devastation. While evacuating your family can be a real hassle, so can being stranded on your roof for days, doing Sudoku puzzles and hoping the city comes by to rescue you soon. In other words, err on the side of caution. Better to be that guy who spends a night at a Motel 6 eating pizza and watching news reports as the storm totally misses his city.

PLAN AHEAD Sit down with your family (or roommates or cats) and agree where you'll meet up if the storm strikes while some of you are at work or school or otherwise away from home.

TOP OFF Fill up your gas tank every time it gets close to the half-empty mark during storm season, and even more frequently if a storm is imminent. Gas will likely run out as all those less-prepared people storm the pumps. Also, if the power goes, those pumps won't work anyway. Buy two gas cans way before storm season starts.

LIVE READY Keep "go bags" stocked for each family member, and any pets you'd be evacuating with you, holding a change of clothes, some high-energy snacks (you may not be able to stop for a bite for some time), basic toiletries, glasses or contacts, and any prescription medicines.

USE PAPER Be sure you have paper maps of the area in your car. You'll probably be able to rely on GPS navigation, but it just makes sense to have a backup, especially since your usual routes may be closed, flooded, or packed bumper to bumper.

CARRY CASH If the power goes down, ATMs and pay-point machines won't work. Keep a wad of cash hidden but easy to get to if you're dashing out of the home.

The tropical cyclone with the highest wind speeds ever measured was Tropical Cyclone Olivia, which struck Australia in 1996. It had wind speeds of 253 MPH, which are still the fastest non-tornado winds ever measured on the surface of the Earth. Luckily, the storm's path took it through relatively undeveloped areas, so it did not cause any fatalities, although ten people were injured.

155 MAKE A PLAN

☐ Go over the hurricane warning system, and what to do if it sounds when the household's not together.

☐ Discuss plans for anyone with special needs, including infants, disabled people, the elderly, and pets. Try to anticipate and prepare for challenges. Consider e-mailing a copy of the plan to all members of the household, or use cloud storage for easy access on any computer or device.

☐ Determine at least two home-escape routes in case your home is hit hard, and agree upon a muster point outside the home. Look at local hurricane maps and plan evacuation routes and where to meet if you get separated.

☐ Develop an emergency communication plan. Ask an out-of-town relative or friend to be your "family contact" to coordinate communication in case other communication means fail. If unable to reach one another, family members should call the contact and tell that person where they are and how they're doing. Include the contact's name, address, e-mail, and phone number in your plan.

In order for a plan to be effective during a real disaster when things will be chaotic, you'll need to regularly review and update the details with your entire family. That way, everyone will reflexively remember and follow the steps during an actual emergency.

DENNIS DEBUNKS:
LADY STORMS GET NO RESPECT

A recent study claimed that storms with female names cause more fatalities than those with male names because people subconsciously feel like a storm named "Debby" couldn't possibly be as dangerous as one called "Tony," for example. While it's true that there have been more deadly storms with female names, male names were only added in 1979, which skews the data.

156 COOK UP A CYCLONE

When one side of the world starts to feel the heat of the sun during the summer season, it's not just the atmosphere that warms up. The sun's rays also slowly heat up the water in the oceans, allowing their surfaces to get as hot as 90° F in places. This excessive warmth does more than confuse swimmers who wanted to take a refreshing dip—it also alters the weather.

Just like any organized weather system (or delicious cake), hurricanes need the right ingredients to come together at just the right moment. To cook up a hurricane, you need the following four major ingredients.

1. A NUCLEUS Even the most powerful hurricanes can form from a feature as small as a few city blocks. A tropical system requires a nucleus for development, which can be anything from a complex of thunderstorms that rolls offshore to a trough of low pressure, or even the remnants of an old storm that's fizzled out.

2. WARM WATER Sea surface temperatures are a critical factor in the life cycle of a tropical cyclone. The air just above the surface of the ocean is heated by the ocean itself, so warm water fosters warm air, which naturally rises and feeds the growing cyclone and storm system. As a result, tropical systems weaken considerably once they move over cooler water.

3. MOISTURE Hurricanes need to form in environments rich in moisture. After all, they are by definition moist tropical entities. Limited moisture inhibits thunderstorm development, choking the storm and forcing it to shrivel up and fizzle out.

4. LOW WIND SHEAR Wind shear is fatal to tropical cyclones—strong winds in the mid or upper levels of the atmosphere can shear the tops off of thunderstorms that try to form the storm's eye, preventing the tropical cyclone from getting its act together.

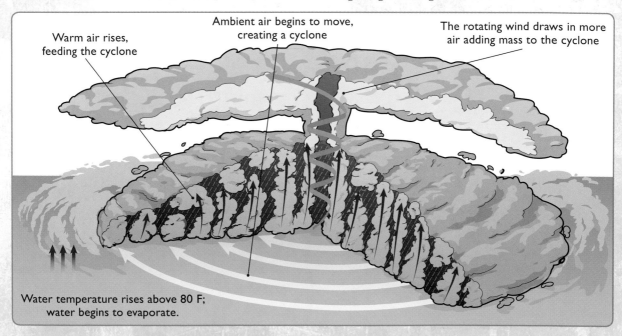

Warm air rises, feeding the cyclone

Ambient air begins to move, creating a cyclone

The rotating wind draws in more air adding mass to the cyclone

Water temperature rises above 80 F; water begins to evaporate.

157 LOOK IT IN THE EYE

The most prominent and important features of a hurricane are the eye and its associated eyewall. Remember that all weather occurs as a result of nature trying to achieve balance throughout the world; in other words, if you remove air from one spot, more air will rush in to fill the empty space. The eye of a hurricane forms because air from the upper levels of the atmosphere sinks through the center of the storm in a futile attempt to fill the storm's extremely deep low pressure and bring the atmosphere back to normal. In perfect circumstances, weather conditions in the eye are strangely calm, with no precipitation or wind.

The eye is surrounded by the eyewall, which is the most intense part of a hurricane. The eyewall is the engine that keeps the storm chugging along—air rising from the ocean's surface feeds the intense thunderstorm activity in the eyewall, allowing the storm to maintain its strength and organization. Sustained winds in the eyewall can reach speeds of nearly 200 MPH, with gusts of nearly 250 MPH.

When you look at satellite imagery, you can diagnose the health of a hurricane by looking at both its eye and a feature called the "central dense overcast," or the large, solid mass of clouds that surrounds the eye. Well-organized storms feature a thick, healthy central dense overcast, while wind shear and dry air filtering into the storm can cause the central dense overcast to fall apart or develop streaks, indicating potential weakening.

Finally, there are the rain bands that give hurricanes their classic buzz-saw appearance. Rain bands are the usually the first taste of the storm, featuring squally weather with bursts of heavy rain and gusty winds. Then the bulk of the hurricane moves overhead, and you're in for what seems like an eternity of the worst nature can throw at you.

158 KNOW THE SEASON

Nature tends to schedule certain events consistently, which gives us a pretty good idea of when certain types of weather will occur. The most common time for dangerous severe thunderstorm outbreaks in the United States, for instance, is around April and May, while most areas close to the poles will reliably see heavy snowfall during the dead of winter. The time of the year when tropical cyclones typically form is known as "hurricane season," but the time frames differ dramatically around the world.

NORTH AMERICA In the Atlantic Ocean, hurricane season runs from June 1 through November 30. Almost every tropical storm in history has formed in this six-month period, though some have popped up as early as April or as late as December. Hurricane season off the western coast of North America starts just a bit earlier—May 15—thanks to warmer waters and generally favorable conditions. Favorable to the scary storms, that is.

OCEANIA Cyclone season around Australia and New Zealand is similar to what folks in North America have to deal with, but on a mirrored timetable due to the difference in seasons between the hemispheres. Cyclone season in the land down under begins in the beginning of November, and runs through the end of April.

EVERYWHERE ELSE Hurricane season elsewhere is a bit trickier to define. Typhoons in the western Pacific Ocean and cyclones in the Indian Ocean can occur year-round, so these basins don't have a defined season like we see in the Atlantic. However, typhoons and cyclones in these regions are most common during the heat of the summer months. Typhoon activity during the off months is more common close to the equator, where air temperatures stay at a steady, muggy level the entire year. One of the deadliest typhoons in history struck during the off months: Super Typhoon Haiyan swept through the Philippines in the middle of November 2013.

159 WATCH THOSE WARNINGS

As with tornadoes (see item 106), there are several levels of alerts issued when conditions are conducive to a tropical storm or hurricane forming. Here's the breakdown, and what to do when you hear them issued.

STORM WATCH A tropical storm or hurricane watch simply means that a storm is possible in your area under the current conditions. When you hear a storm watch has been issued, it's a good idea to check your emergency supplies, make sure your family's go bags are packed, and check that everyone remembers the evacuation and meet-up plan. Check your home's exterior and be sure it's as windproof as possible (see item 131). Storm watches tend to be issued 48 hours before winds are expected to kick it into high gear, so get that patio furniture stowed away first.

STORM WARNING The jump from "watch" to "warning" is the jump from "possible" to "expected." The agency issuing the alert estimates winds will reach high levels within 36 hours. This is when evacuation orders will likely begin. Those who don't dally reap the benefits of less traffic, better supplies, and the bonus of not being stuck in a hurricane that they ignored until the last minute.

EXTREME WIND WARNING Extreme sustained winds associated with a major hurricane (115 MPH or greater), are expected to begin within an hour. Take immediate shelter in the safest spot you can reach.

EXTREME WEATHER HISTORY:
TYPHOON HAIYAN

The last place you want to have to ride out a hurricane is on an island, yet so many tropical islands are sitting ducks for cyclone activity. One of the worst storms in recent memory crashed ashore in the Philippines on November 7, 2013, leaving in its wake the worst weather disaster in the country's modern history.

Typhoon Haiyan took advantage of an optimal environment and formed into a monster, cementing its status as one of the strongest storms on record, with one-minute sustained winds of 195 MPH. Usually when a storm this strong gets going over the ocean, it peaks away from land and weakens before making landfall. In this case, unfortunately, Haiyan made landfall near Tacloban City at maximum strength, becoming the strongest tropical cyclone ever recorded on landfall.

Haiyan's winds were bad enough, but the surge that accompanied the storm was devastating. Tacloban City sits at the base of a funnel-shaped bay, and it also found itself on the northern side of the storm's eyewall, shoving unimaginable amounts of water into the bay and virtually destroying the city with winds and flooding.

By the time the storm cleared out, residents discovered that more than 6,000 of their fellow citizens had lost their lives as a result of the storm, and tens of thousands more were homeless and lacking the basic supplies required to live. Thankfully, storms as strong as Haiyan are rare, but when one makes landfall in a heavily populated country like the Philippines, the destruction can be utterly catastrophic.

160 GET OUT OF DODGE

We've talked a lot about evacuation. Now it's time to do it. Your local government has declared that a major hurricane is coming and people in your area need to get to safety. What now?

FOLLOW THE PLAN Remember that communication and evacuation plan you made with your family? Now's the time to put it to use. That already puts you ahead of the vast majority of your fellow citizens, who are either ignoring the sirens or desperately trying to find that rusty old gas can in the basement.

BRING A BACKUP Keep photocopies of all your crucial documents (passports, credit cards, Social Security cards, insurance paperwork) in a waterproof envelope in a file cabinet or desk drawer, easy to grab and go when the time comes.

MAKE THE CALL If you're not fleeing for your life, try and take the time to call or e-mail your out-of-state family contact and let him know your plans. Leave a note in your home with contact information and your immediate plans in case anyone is looking for you.

PULL THE PLUG Unplug all of your electronics except for the fridge and freezer (and unplug those as well if there's a danger your house might flood). Bring perishables with you for road food.

SNAP A SHOT If the storm is predicted to be a big one, snap some pictures of your home's interior and exterior in case you need to make insurance claims.

LEND A HAND If you have space, offer neighbors a ride. If you don't, ask if there's anyone you can contact for them if the situation gets worse.

162
EVACUATE RIGHT

You had a plan and the plan worked. While other citizens of your town are ignoring the weather reports or banging on the Home Depot's doors demanding clear plastic and duct tape RIGHT NOW, you've got the family loaded into your car and are headed to safety. The hints here will just make that journey a little more pleasant.

STOCK UP Be prepared to spend at least 12 hours on the road (this will of course vary widely depending on the region and the storm, but as guidelines go, it's a pretty good one). Be sure you have snacks, water, caffeine, and car chargers for all of your devices. If you have young kids, bring some of their favorite toys and games to distract them in this stressful time.

BE ALERT In a big storm, road conditions may change quickly, and posting warnings may not be a priority. It's on you to keep your eyes open for washed-out roads, rickety bridges, and downed power lines. If you see standing water in the road, don't assume it's shallow. Every year cars get submerged up to their window frames because some little puddle grew massively overnight.

PLAN FOR PETS Of course you should take your pets with you if they would otherwise be in danger, but do be aware that they may not be allowed in disaster relief shelters with you. Before disaster strikes, have a plan for them, perhaps an out-of-town friend or family member who would be willing to care for them until you return home.

161
DON'T RELAX

It's true that things are often calm or very nearly calm in the eye of a hurricane. But don't let your guard down, and don't let the light breeze, lack of precipitation, and even sunny skies fool you—once the other side of the eyewall reaches your location, conditions will go from calm to calamity in just a couple of minutes, posing a grave threat to anyone outdoors and unprotected. In many ways, the trailing winds are even more dangerous, since all the loose debris that blew one way will come flying back in the other direction.

KNOW THE TRUTH
HURRICANES

When you take a worldwide weather event as destructive and far-reaching as a hurricane, it'd be disappointing if there weren't all sorts of folk wisdom and just plain crazy talk about it. Which of the following stories are true and which aren't? Read on.

HEAD NORTH TO EVADE HURRICANES

If you talk to folks in places like New England and Canada, they'll tell you that above certain latitudes, hurricanes are just tuckered out from their long sprint to the poles, and can't do any more damage.

FALSE This isn't just wrong, it's dangerously wrong, if it means people don't think they need to worry about being prepared. Just look at storms like 2012's Hurricane Sandy; 2003's Hurricane Juan, which devastated parts of Atlantic Canada; and the "Long Island Express" hurricane of 1939, which made landfall on Long Island as a Category 3 storm and moved into New England shortly thereafter. Complacency like this makes storms that hit unusual areas especially dangerous.

OKAY, FINE, HEAD INLAND THEN

Hurricanes hit beaches hard, venting a lot of their pent-up fury along whatever coast they're battering. The coast serves as a front line, protecting the inland areas by absorbing the worst of it.

TRUE (to a degree) If you live on the coast and evacuate ahead of an approaching hurricane, you're safe from the worst of the winds and storm surge, but maybe not from all of the storm's effects. Many inland locations are slammed by high winds, rains, and tornadoes as a storm pushes its way ashore. For example, in 1989's Hurricane Hugo, buildings in Charlotte, North Carolina were heavily damaged and some people lost power for weeks, even though the city is nearly 200 miles from the coast.

TAPE UP YOUR WINDOWS

When high winds threaten, people without storm shutters fear having their windows shatter. To prevent the glass breaking, all you have to do is place strips of tape across the windowpanes.

FALSE Taping a window doesn't stop the glass from breaking—it just keeps the window from breaking into smaller pieces. The tape only holds together the jagged shards of glass; instead of having 700 bits of glass to clean up, you only have 50 larger pieces. Which is something, but isn't as good as having unbroken windows. Boarding up windows with plywood is the best way to protect them from flying debris.

FINE, THEN, LEAVE THEM OPEN

Hurricanes involve massive pressure differentials—that's where they get their awesome and often terrifying power. So it just makes sense that subjecting a sealed environment to that kind of pressure could blow it to bits . . . right? The only sensible thing to do is to leave a window open so that the low pressure outside doesn't cause your house to explode.

FALSE That's just wrong. It's the wind and flooding that destroy a house during a tropical cyclone, not the pressure difference. Opening your windows just makes it easier for the wind to get into your house and tear it apart from the inside out.

IT'S NOT THE SIZE, IT'S WHAT YOU DO WITH IT

You'd think that physics would dictate a fairly clear correlation. Big storms = lots of energy = major carnage. Smaller storms, the reverse. But in fact, while size does matter to an extent, you can't always judge a tropical cyclone by its size.

TRUE The smallest storms can pack a mean punch, and some of the biggest do very little. The only time a cyclone's size matters is in determining how many locations will feel its effects. Hurricane Sandy was so destructive because its wind field was so large—high winds extended nearly 500 miles from the center at landfall. On the flip side, Cyclone Tracy devastated Darwin, Australia, even though the entire storm was just over two dozen miles across.

EXTREME WEATHER HISTORY:
HURRICANE KATRINA

The most devastating hurricane to hit the United States in modern history was Hurricane Katrina, which tore its way inland from the northern Gulf Coast on August 29, 2005. The hurricane peaked in strength with winds of 175 MPH shortly before landfall, but weakened somewhat before its eyewall raked the coastal regions of Louisiana, Mississippi, and Alabama.

When people talk about Hurricane Katrina today, few people talk about the damage produced by the winds. The big story in Katrina was the storm surge, or the surge of water pushed inland by the storm's strong winds. Pass Christian, Mississippi, saw the highest storm surge ever recorded in the United States, with the water reaching a maximum depth of nearly 28 feet along the coast. The water acted like a bulldozer, demolishing almost every structure in its path.

Katrina's path was the worst-case scenario for New Orleans, a city of nearly half a million people (at the time) that sits a few feet below sea level. Residents of New Orleans are protected from the surrounding water by an intricate system of levees, or walls that keep the city from being submerged. The extreme storm surge in Katrina pushed more water into local waterways than the levees could handle, causing many of these man-made structures to fail, allowing water to pour into the city. Nearly 2,000 people died when Katrina made landfall, almost all of whom drowned when the waters inundated New Orleans and surrounding areas.

163 FEAR THE ATLANTIC MONSTER

Monstrous, iconic Atlantic storms typically form in the second half of summer, with the climatological peak in hurricane activity occurring on September 10. Almost all of the United States's historic storms—Katrina, Ivan, Andrew, Ike, Camille—formed in August or September. These hurricanes are particularly long-lived, forming near the Cape Verde Islands just off the western coast of Africa. The early organization of these systems gives them more than a week to traverse the warm waters of the Atlantic before they threaten land, allowing them to grow into some of the strongest storms ever recorded.

Heading south of the equator, as in the southeastern Pacific Ocean, cooler waters and generally unfavorable winds tend to inhibit tropical cyclone activity in the southern Atlantic Ocean. While rare, tropical and subtropical storms have formed off the coast of Brazil. Through the course of recorded history, only one hurricane has ever formed in the southern Atlantic Ocean. Hurricane Catarina developed in March 2004 as a Category 2 storm with winds of 100 MPH, killing several people and causing hundreds of millions of dollars in damage when it made landfall in southeastern Brazil.

164 THROW A RESCUE ROPE

We've seen it in the movies a thousand times . . . someone is about to be swept away by raging floodwaters when— huzzah!—a heroic type throws him a rope and hauls him to safety. The only problem with this is, unless you're tossing the rope directly down to someone, it doesn't have the heft to be hurled very far. The answer is to tie this big, bulky knot, which serves two complementary purposes. First, it weights the rope so that it's easier to throw. Secondly, it gives the person being rescued something substantial to hang onto while being hauled from the water.

STEP 1 Make two open-ended U-shaped loops at the end of the rope (these loops are called "bights"). This results in three "rungs" of rope lined up on your surface.

STEP 2 Weave the end of the rope under the middle rung and over the bottom one (A). Then loop it around the back of the knot and bring it between the top and middle rungs.

STEP 3 Wrap all rungs six to nine times. On the last wrap, thread the working end of the rope through the loop (B).

STEP 4 Tighten by pulling on the standing end of the line and on the bights on each end of the knot (C).

STEP 5 To throw the rope, stack it at your feet starting with the end you'll be holding so that it uncoils tangle-free.

165 NEVER TRY TO OUTRUN THE SURGE

While water is surging ashore, your options are very limited. Basically, get to the highest point you can and hope it's higher than the peak of the surge. In Hurricane Katrina, some people drowned in their homes because the surge filled the rooms so quickly that they couldn't escape. Water can rise 6 to 10 feet in minutes—faster if it's filling an enclosed space.

Still, it's common for people to try to outrun the surge in their cars. The logic behind this mistake is thinking that since it's no problem to drive through an inch of water, as long as you drive fast enough, you can get away before it rises any higher.

The fact is that if you wait until the water is an inch high before trying to outrun the surge, it will likely rise to over a foot high before you can even get your car out of the driveway. If the water is a foot high and traveling at 10 to 15 miles per hour, it can easily sweep a car away. Don't risk it.

166 DON'T GO UNDER

Wind speeds sound dramatic, but the storm surge is the more lethal threat. A storm surge occurs when a hurricane's winds push ocean water onto land, creating a flood that can be tens of feet deep and reach several miles inland. If you've ever watched strong winds blow across the surface of a pool or a pond, you can see the small waves focus their energy on one end of the body of water. If the winds are strong enough, you can even see the small waves push over the edge of the pool or pond.

BIG BLOW Tropical cyclones can have wind fields that extend more than 100 miles from the storm's center—this mass of violent winds takes a great toll on the surface of the ocean, pushing along a bubble-like surge of water ahead of it. When the cyclone makes landfall, this bubble of water piles up on the coast and starts to push inland. Most storm surges rise from nothing to a catastrophe in a matter of hours, and the vast majority of people who die from hurricanes in the United States die as a direct result of storm surges.

TINY TERROR Even marginal tropical storms can produce a small storm surge, the effects of which vary widely depending on a number of factors. Most surges are only a few feet deep, affecting communities immediately along the coast, but one storm hitting the wrong area can wreak havoc. Hurricane Sandy is an example of this—even though it only had winds of about 80 MPH at landfall, its wind field was so large that it pushed a devastating storm surge into the U.S. East Coast, especially in and around New York City.

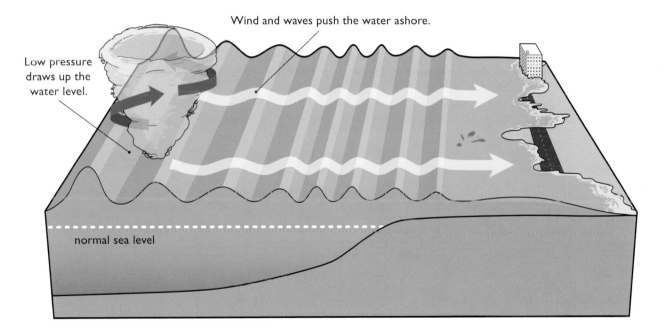

Wind and waves push the water ashore.

Low pressure draws up the water level.

normal sea level

167 PREPARE FOR FLOODING

Beyond the wind and storm surge that whip through coastal communities during a hurricane, storms remain a threat as they push ashore and weaken to what's known as a remnant low. Stronger storms don't immediately lose their strength, with some maintaining tropical storm or hurricane status up to 100 miles inland.

The greatest threat that accompanies a storm making its way inland is flooding from heavy rainfall. The remnant of a hurricane can produce unbelievable amounts of rain, with more than 2 feet of rain not uncommon in especially juicy or slow-moving systems. Some of the worst flooding disasters in American history occurred as a result of remnant hurricanes, and these catastrophes happen with some regularity in mountainous countries like Mexico, where high terrain enhances precipitation and leads to lethal mudslides and flash floods.

It's good to remember that flooding is flooding, whether it's from a stalled thunderstorm or the last gasps of a once-mighty hurricane, and you should take the same precautions as you would during any other flooding event (such as not driving through high water, and preparing to move to higher ground).

168 DEAL WITH A FLOODED BASEMENT

A flooded basement is not only a hassle, it's potentially fatal. If there is any standing water, assume it's now a dangerous electrical hazard. Before venturing in, make sure it's safe by having an electrician turn off the power at the meter (this is much safer than just turning off circuits, but must be done by a professional). If there are any gas appliances in the basement, shut off the gas main until the basement has been cleared.

Once it's safe to enter the basement, the easiest way to drain it is to rent a pump or have a service do it for you. There will likely be extensive property damage, and the risk of mold means that you'll need to properly dehumidify and rehabilitate the space. This can be complex, time-consuming, and expensive. If you don't have the experience to handle it right, hire professionals.

To prevent or limit damage, protect your property by placing it on shelves in watertight containers. Keep non-waterproof items at least 3 inches off the floor so that water seeping in cannot damage them.

Install any electrical outlets and equipment high up and elevate the main breaker or fuse box and the utility meters above the anticipated flood level. Install ground-fault interrupter (GFI) outlets as required by code, and don't leave extension cords on the floor.

169 FACE THE AFTERMATH

Once you've been so fortunate as to survive the fury of a land falling hurricane, the danger is far from over. Survivors will potentially face uninhabitable homes, no utilities, poor hygiene, and likely low or no supplies of food and water. Emergency responders will have a hard time wading through the debris to save and evacuate survivors. Hopefully, you were able to evacuate in time. If so, don't return until authorities say that it's safe to do so.

INFRASTRUCTURE ISSUES You never realize how much you take basic necessities like electricity and running water for granted until these services are interrupted. Outages can last weeks or even months after a particularly destructive hurricane. Damage to infrastructure (and lack of electricity at municipal stations) causes similar disruptions to water and sewage systems, preventing you from flushing the toilet, washing your hands, bathing, or even cooking. Once the water does come back, don't drink it until local authorities say it's safe—there are all kinds of disgusting things that might be wrong (see item 145).

CLEANUP COSTS It is insanely expensive to stave off rising floodwaters and endure the daunting task of cleaning up after one of these torrents of water. A year of bad flooding can directly cause billions of dollars in damage and prevention/cleanup efforts. The indirect costs can be millions more, from ruined crops, shuttered factories, and the homes and businesses destroyed (and people displaced) by the floodwaters. One bad flood can irreparably devastate a small town, so brace yourself for bad news.

170 PREGAME YOUR PLYWOOD

Do you own a house that's frequently in the path of heavy weather? There are little hacks you can do to simplify the inevitable girding for a storm. Cut pieces of plywood to fit perfectly over doors and windows, and then carefully label them with waterproof pen and store them in a logical order in your basement or garage so there's no guesswork or delay when the storm warning goes out. Also, you can install subtle fasteners and brackets on the outside of window frames to make boarding the place up something that takes minutes, not hours, and can be done by less-handy members of the household.

171 WATCH THE WATER

Flooding can do more than simply sweep away homes and vehicles like they were twigs in front of a garden hose. Residents cleaning up from floods can end up grappling with economic losses, mold, chemicals, and even some unfriendly visitors.

It is insanely expensive to stave off rising floodwaters and endure the daunting task of cleaning up after one of these torrents of water. One year of bad flooding can directly cost billions of dollars in damage and prevention/cleanup efforts. The indirect costs can be millions more, from ruined crops, shuttered factories, and the homes and businesses destroyed (and people displaced) by the floodwaters. One bad flood can irreparably devastate a small town.

Water isn't the only thing you have to worry about when towns are threatened by rivers overflowing their banks. The brown, murky liquid isn't always just water—it's raw sewage, toxic chemicals, oil, gasoline, medicine, and just about every other nasty, lethal thing you can think of, all mixed into one horrible slurry. Oh, and don't forget all of the ants, spiders, snakes, and other unfriendly creatures that are displaced. They can cling to any floating debris, providing an unwelcome surprise to anyone who finds themselves wading through the ick.

Those who are lucky enough to have homes to return to once the waters recede can find some ugly surprises on the walls. Mold is a huge and costly issue that plagues buildings after a flood; the mold is even worse if the water was especially deep or the flood occurred during the warmer months. The mold can be so thick and toxic that some homes are torn down because the task of removing it is too costly (or just downright dangerous).

172
HUNKER DOWN AT HOME

If you decide not to evacuate, at least make that decision in advance and stick with it. Many preventable injuries and deaths in these situations come when someone who had planned to ride out the storm at home suddenly panics and decides to head for an emergency shelter. Be sure your home emergency kit is up to date (see item 16).

It's far too dangerous to attempt to drive to an evacuation center in high winds: the roads may be impassible due to high water at bridges or flooded underpasses, or they may be obstructed by fallen power poles—and your vehicle can provide little protection from flying debris carried by 100-MPH winds.

In deciding whether or not to stay, be aware of factors that make your house vulnerable to a hurricane's effects. If it's built on a ridge and exposed to high winds, or in a valley, alongside a river or stream, or in a storm-surge zone, you might want to get out of town.

If you choose not to evacuate, but your roof blows away, remain inside. Shelter in the smallest interior room in your house, likely a bathroom or a closet, which offers the greatest strength and protection from flying debris.

173
DON'T GET BLOWN AWAY

Some of the strongest hurricanes produce winds equivalent to what you'd see in a powerful tornado, just over a much, much larger area. A Category 5 hurricane can pack the same intensity as a high-end EF-3 tornado, but over dozens of miles instead of a few thousand feet.

FALLING TREES The damage caused by winds increases steadily with greater speed. A pocket of 80-MPH sustained winds will result in less damage than 140 MPH winds, of course, but each is dangerous if your home is in the path of a tree that comes crashing to the ground. Trees can withstand a surprising amount of force, but their ability to stand up to a hurricane depends on a range of factors such as height, foliage, root systems, soil moisture, and tree health. If you live in a building surrounded by tall trees, it would be a good idea to evacuate to safer shelter if you can.

STRUCTURAL DAMAGE The most serious wind damage occurs to buildings. Damage is highly dependent on how well the building is constructed—modern school buildings, for instance, can withstand much higher winds than single-family homes. Weaker hurricanes cause mostly superficial damage, such as tearing off vinyl siding and roof shingles, but otherwise don't compromise the integrity of the building. Damage to gabled roofs and garages can facilitate the destruction of the building—if garage doors fail, wind can get into the garage and tear it apart from the inside out, compromising the rest of the house. Similar damage can occur when a roof fails, weakening the structure and allowing damaging winds to more easily tear away at walls and support beams.

WIND-BORNE PERIL Flying debris is a significant threat to those caught outside during strong winds. Never venture outside during a hurricane, even if you think it's safe to do so. It just takes one small, flying object nailing you just right to make you wish you had stayed inside.

EXTREME WEATHER HISTORY:
GALVESTON HURRICANE

Even with all of the modern technologies we have at our fingertips, powerful storms can still claim countless lives if they hit the wrong place at the wrong time. However, high casualty rates were the norm before we developed things like weather radar, satellite imagery, and even things as simple as automated electronic weather stations. One storm that predates modern technology was especially cruel, even by the standards of the day: The Galveston Hurricane of 1900 was and still is the deadliest natural disaster to ever strike the United States.

A few dozen miles to the southeast of Houston, the growing city of Galveston, Texas, sits just off the coast on a barrier island in the Gulf of Mexico. The city's location leaves it vulnerable to any tropical system that makes its way northwest toward the Lone Star State, and this was especially true in the early 20th century. An intense Category 4 hurricane rapidly organized itself in the Gulf of Mexico, taking direct aim at Galveston.

Residents had little to no warning that a hurricane was approaching the city. The strong winds, heavy rain, and rising waters smacked the island on September 8, 1900; estimated winds in the unnamed hurricane were well over 100 MPH at landfall. A 15-foot storm surge engulfed Galveston Island, completely washing over the landmass and destroying almost every building.

Survivors were never able to get an accurate death toll, since many of the bodies had washed away, but most researchers agree that more than 6,000 people were killed in Galveston alone, with some estimates putting the total at more than 10,000.

174 BEWARE THE STEALTH TWISTER

Moving from the ground back to the sky, one of the most overlooked threats during a hurricane is a tornado, which really adds insult to injury when you think about it. Small tornadoes are common in the fast-moving bands of showers and thunderstorms as they push ashore, resulting from the incredible amounts of low-level wind shear and rotation that can accompany tropical systems. Tornado outbreaks are common in storms that make landfall on the United States' Gulf Coast—several days after making landfall in Florida, 2004's Hurricane Ivan produced more than one hundred tornadoes as it moved up the East Coast, killing several people and causing tens of millions of dollars in damage.

175 DRIVE ON FLOODED STREETS

The most basic rule for driving through flooded streets is—don't. However, if you're in a situation where you either think it's worth the risk, or feel fairly confident that the water isn't that bad, here are some guidelines for what is likely to be a bad decision.

Start by scanning the flooded area really well, to be sure the water isn't too deep. You'll want to turn off the air conditioning, to help avoid getting damaging water drawn into the fan in the engine compartment. Downshift to your lowest possible gear, and drive very slowly and carefully through the area.

Keep the engine revving, as you don't want to stall out in the water. Once you exit the water, pump your brakes to help dry the brake pads, and be aware that your brakes won't respond as well once they're wet. As soon as you can, have a mechanic check your car out, as water damage to the engine or the interior might cause issues later.

EXTREME WEATHER AROUND THE WORLD:
AUSTRALIA

With overgrown snakes, scorpions galore, deadly sea creatures, and some of the hottest temperatures attainable without hurling yourself into a volcano, it truly seems like the environment in Australia is trying to kill you. And regular tropical cyclone activity is just the icing on the poison cake.

Since cyclones move poleward (in this case, from north to south), the northern half of Australia faces the greatest threat from tropical cyclones, particularly the northwestern part of the country. Darwin is the largest city at risk for tropical cyclones in Australia; the city was virtually wiped out when Cyclone Tracy, an exceptionally small and intense storm, made a direct strike on Christmas Day in 1974. Fortunately, Darwin has since recovered and grown to nearly four times its original size.

176 TACKLE WATER DAMAGE

If your home has suffered water damage from flooding, it will be prone to a mold infestation, which can develop after only 24–48 hours of water exposure.

DRY OUT Set up fans and dehumidifiers, and move wet items away from walls and off the floors. Find the source of the moisture and stop it from worsening the problem.

TOSS THE TRASH Items that have absorbed moisture and have mold growing on them need to be thrown out. Remove the sheetrock a level above the high-water mark of any flooding. Any porous material that shows visible signs of mold should be thrown away.

CLEAN UP Surface mold growing on nonporous materials can usually be cleaned. Thoroughly scrub contaminated surfaces with hot water, a non-ammonia soap, detergent, or commercial cleaner. Use a stiff brush to scrub out all contaminants. Rinse with clean water and collect the excess rinse water and detergent with a wet/dry vacuum, a mop, or a sponge.

DISINFECT Apply a bleach solution or antimicrobial cleaner to surfaces that show mold growth. An effective

way to eliminate mold and musty smells in large or inaccessible spaces is to use a "cold fogger," which distributes a mold-control mist evenly throughout the living space, even in hard-to-access areas.

LOOK OUT Be alert to the signs of mold returning to areas of past infestation. If it does return, repeat cleaning steps or, in cases of heavy infestation, seek professional help. Regrowth is usually a sign that the moisture has not been controlled effectively.

177 KNOW YOUR MONSOONS

"Oh, man, it's a monsoon out there!" We like to talk about extremely heavy rain by calling it a "monsoon" because it just sounds so much cooler than calling it a heavy rainstorm. The widespread abuse of this term (at least in the United States) is largely due to the fact that we don't have to deal with monsoons much around these parts.

Monsoons aren't storms at all, but rather large-scale weather patterns that set up over certain parts of the world. A monsoon is colloquially known as a rainy season, when warmer and wetter air flows inland, allowing persistent heavy rains to develop and drench a region in glorious liquid sunshine. Monsoons are most common in warmer climates like the Indian subcontinent, or desert regions like the American Southwest.

The process that creates monsoonal flow is essentially a giant sea breeze; the land heats up faster than the water, heating the air over the land and causing it to rise. The cooler air over the water rushes in to fill the void, creating a moist onshore flow that helps produce heavy rain and thunderstorms.

Out of all of the regions that see monsoons, the rain that can fall in parts of the Indian subcontinent is a sight to behold. India and Bangladesh get brutally hot and humid during the summer months, allowing for the heaviest rain on Earth to fall every year like clockwork. In fact, the World Meteorological Organization recognizes Cherrapunji, India, as having seen the most rain ever recorded in one year. Residents of this town near the border of Bangladesh saw 1,042 inches (86.8 feet) of rain between August 1860 and July 1861. Cherrapunji sits near the foot of tall hills and mountains, allowing warm, moist, southerly winds from the Bay of Bengal to blow up against the terrain, forcing clouds to rise and wring water out over the city.

178 CATEGORIZE THAT HURRICANE

We love to use scales to figure out how one major disaster compares to others in objective terms. It's one thing to say that a hurricane had 145 MPH winds, but when you instead say, "The hurricane was a Category 4," locals instantly get an idea of what kind of damage the winds could produce. The Saffir-Simpson Hurricane Wind Scale was introduced in the mid 1970s by Herbert Saffir and Robert Simpson in order to estimate the amount of damage a hurricane could be expected to produce on landfall. Just based on winds, a Category 1 hurricane would cause much less damage than a Category 5.

While the Saffir-Simpson scale is a useful tool for quickly and effectively communicating hurricane risk to the public, it does have its disadvantages. Winds are only part of the equation—residents who are facing (and trying to evaluate) the threat of a hurricane have to take into account the risk for flooding and/or a storm surge, as well as the possibility of tornadoes in addition to the winds. Hurricane Sandy was "only" a Category 1 when it made landfall in the northeastern United States, but its immense storm surge devastated hundreds of miles of coastline from New Jersey to Rhode Island.

CATEGORY 1
WIND SPEEDS: 74–95 MPH
EXPECTED DAMAGE:
Widespread
TYPE OF DAMAGE:
Branches and limbs down, damage to gutters, shingles, and siding.
EXAMPLE (STRENGTH AT LANDFALL):
Hurricane Irene (2011)

CATEGORY 2
WIND SPEEDS: 96–110 MPH
EXPECTED DAMAGE:
Severe
TYPE OF DAMAGE:
Widespread roof damage occurs; extensive power outages.
EXAMPLE (STRENGTH AT LANDFALL):
Hurricane Arthur (2014)

CATEGORY 3
WIND SPEEDS: 111–129 MPH
EXPECTED DAMAGE:
Extreme
TYPE OF DAMAGE:
Most buildings damaged, some homes destroyed.
EXAMPLE (STRENGTH AT LANDFALL):
Hurricane Katrina (2005)

CATEGORY 4
WIND SPEEDS: 130–156 MPH
EXPECTED DAMAGE:
Catastrophic
TYPE OF DAMAGE:
Most buildings damaged, some homes destroyed.
EXAMPLE (STRENGTH AT LANDFALL):
Hurricane Charley (2004)

CATEGORY 5
WIND SPEEDS: 157+ MPH
EXPECTED DAMAGE:
Complete devastation
TYPE OF DAMAGE:
Equivalent to a violent tornado. Devastation likely. Area uninhabitable for an extended period of time.
EXAMPLE (STRENGTH AT LANDFALL):
Hurricane Andrew (1992)

1995 CHICAGO HEAT WAVE

When we think about natural disasters, the exciting stuff is always at the top of the list: tornadoes, hurricanes, tsunamis, earthquakes. Injuries and fatalities from extreme temperatures are overlooked because their effects aren't always immediately obvious to everyone. Heat is truly a silent killer, and residents of Chicago, Illinois, learned this lesson all too well during the mid 1990s.

During the third week of July 1995, a potent ridge of high pressure developed over the eastern United States, focusing a large amount of heat and humidity on the Midwest. Chicago was the largest city affected by the ensuing heat wave, where high temperatures spiked in the 100s, with heat indices approaching the upper 110s at times. Low temperatures were so warm that they offered residents little relief. This heat was unrelenting, dragging on for five days and nights before the ridge broke and milder temperatures filtered into the region.

The brutally hot and humid temperatures that befell the central United States that week wreaked havoc on the most vulnerable residents of the city, and by the end of the heat wave, more than 700 people had died as a result of heat-related illnesses. That is a staggering death toll: The deadliest tornado ever recorded in the United States—the Tri-State Tornado of 1925—"only" killed 695 people. The 1995 disaster put the hazards of extreme temperatures front and center in the minds of city-dwellers around the world, and we haven't since had a repeat of this tragic event.

179 RIDE THE WAVE

The exact threshold for a heat wave differs from country to country, but in the United States, the National Weather Service defines a heat wave as a period of two or more days with excessively warm high temperatures.

Most heat waves are caused by strong ridges of high pressure parking over a region for an extended period of time, allowing calm conditions and sunny skies to gradually bake the area. One infamous cause of heat waves in the United States and Canada is known as the "ring of fire," or a strong high pressure that sets up over the central United States, allowing blazing temperatures and choking humidity to blanket the area for a week or longer, in some cases.

Weather conditions that constitute a heat wave are pretty relative around the world. Europe and western Asia can see death tolls in the hundreds after a heat wave that seems mild compared to what other parts of the world experience—many homes in places like Italy or Russia are not equipped with air conditioners, so residents who are already not accustomed to warmer-than-normal temperatures can succumb to heat pretty quickly during a sustained heat wave.

180 SURVIVE A HEAT WAVE

Trying to stay cool during the summer is harder than staying warm during the winter—you can keep piling on layers of clothes and light as many fires as you want (safely, of course!), but you can only remove so many layers of clothing before the police come and haul you away.

The hottest places in the world are miserable in their own right (it's a dry heat), but warm tropical and subtropical regions have the added displeasure of dealing with a stifling humidity that can make everything worse—even fatal.

Thousands of people around the world die every year due to heat-related illnesses, either due to carelessness or unfortunate circumstances, like elderly people who can't afford air conditioning. Some of the highest death tolls in American history occurred as a direct result of unrelenting heat waves, and it seems like we hear about children dying every week because parents left them in a locked car. Here are a few things to do as the mercury rises.

BE SUN SAVVY Open windows on the shady side of the house. On the sunny side of the house, hang exterior shades to block sun from hitting the windows.

PROMOTE CIRCULATION Open the doors and set battery-operated box fans in each entry. They'll expel hot air while drawing cooler air inside.

STAY LOW Remember the old adage about hot air rising? Now's the time that tip comes in handy. Keep to your home's lowest level, where the air is coolest.

GET WET Soak your feet in a basin of water, and wear a damp bandanna around your head. If you have one, fill a spray bottle with water and give yourself a cooling spritz every so often.

DRINK UP Make sure you're getting lots of water, and slow down to reduce perspiration and overheating. Avoid caffeine or alcohol, as they'll just dehydrate you.

UNPLUG IT If your power is on, know that all your household appliances create heat—and that heat really adds up. Unplug computers and lamps with incandescent bulbs, and make meals that don't require heat-generating appliances, such as stoves.

WATCH FOR WARNING SIGNS Know the symptoms of various heat-related illnesses (such as heatstroke and heat exhaustion), and call the authorities if you or a member of your family displays these signs.

181 SURVIVE HEAT ILLNESS

There's heat, and then there's extreme heat—the kind that skyrockets your core body temperature, making you dizzy and hot to the touch. In severe circumstances, heat illness can even be fatal.

HEAT EXHAUSTION The milder of the two heat-related ailments, heat exhaustion occurs when the body's temperature gets too high. People affected experience dizziness, nausea, fatigue, heavy sweating, and clammy skin. The treatment is simple: Have the victim lie down in the shade, elevate his or her feet, and supply plenty of fluids.

HEATSTROKE If a person's core body temperature reaches 104° F, he or she needs immediate treatment for heatstroke, which can be deadly. Besides an alarming thermometer reading, the easiest signs to identify are hot, dry skin; headache; dizziness; and unconsciousness. Heatstroke is a life-threatening emergency and requires immediate treatment in a hospital setting, as it can damage the kidneys, brain, and heart if it goes on for too long at too high a temperature. For transport to the hospital, or if you're waiting for medics, elevate the victim's head and wrap him or her in a wet sheet.

EXTREME WEATHER AROUND THE WORLD: INDIAN OCEAN

The Indian Ocean is a hotbed of cyclone activity when the atmosphere begins to warm up during the summer months, and these storms are especially dangerous because of the poor building quality found in so many locations that surround the ocean basin. Hurricanes take a toll on even the most well-constructed buildings in highly developed countries, so when a powerful storm sweeps inland in a country like Bangladesh, the lives of hundreds of thousands of people are at risk. Unfortunately, this has been the case numerous times throughout recorded history. The deadliest tropical cyclone in world history hit the region now known as Bangladesh; its wind and flooding killed up to 500,000 people. To put that into perspective, Hurricane Katrina in the United States killed about 1,800 people.

182 WATCH OUT FOR CITY HEAT

We've all made this mistake—it's a slow summer afternoon and you're expecting something important in the mail. You're too lazy to throw your shoes on, and the mailbox is right there. You do what any other red-blooded human would do and make a run for it. You realize your mistake the moment you hit the pavement, but it's too late. You can almost hear the sizzle of your foot cooking beneath you.

It's a painful reminder that some surfaces retain heat better than others. Asphalt and concrete warm up much faster than surfaces like mulch and grass, so their temperature (and that of the air just above them) is often much, much hotter than their surroundings. As your feet have surely found out, it's no small difference.

Now, imagine that happening over the entire expanse of a bustling city—all of those cars, hot roofs, brick and concrete facades, and miles upon miles of sidewalks and asphalt roadways, snaking their way from one end of town to the other. These surfaces allow a considerable amount of heat to build up, and it culminates in a very real phenomenon known as the "urban heat island."

The urban heat island effect is a well-documented occurrence seen in most cities (small and large), causing downtown areas to get as much as 5–10° F hotter than the surrounding suburbs. Beyond all of the problems it can cause in recording weather observations, there's a hidden health hazard in this artificial heat.

City centers are often home to a large number of elderly and impoverished citizens, many of whom can't afford simple cooling devices like fans or air conditioning. When a particularly brutal heat wave hits, the urban heat island effect can injure or kill a disproportionate number of people who live in cities, compared to residents of the surrounding areas.

183 EAT RIGHT IN AN OUTAGE

Food can spoil quickly during an extended power outage, and having a plan for how to consume your perishables will keep your family's tummies full and likely free of any food-borne illness. Here is a priority list of what to consume first.

First, use perishable foods from the refrigerator before they spoil. An unopened refrigerator will keep food cold for about 4 hours, so keep the refrigerator doors closed as much as possible.

Next, consume food from the freezer. A full freezer will keep its temperature for about 48 hours (24 hours if it is half full) if the door remains closed.

If it looks like the power outage will continue beyond a day, prepare a camping cooler with ice to hold all of your freezer items.

Use your canned goods, dry goods, and non-perishable foods last, as they will last the longest.

184 DON'T EAT THAT

Is it safe to eat? Throw away any food that has been exposed to temperatures higher than 40° F for 2 hours or more, or that has an unusual odor, color, or texture. Don't rely on taste or appearance to determine its safety.

If food in the freezer is colder than 40° F and has ice crystals on it, you can refreeze it. If you are not sure food is cold enough, take its temperature with a food thermometer.

Some food may look and smell fine, but if it's been at room temperature too long, bacteria that can cause food-borne illnesses may already have contaminated it. When in doubt, throw it out!

WEATHER WORLD RECORDS
HIGHEST TEMPERATURE

The current world-record highest temperature is 134° F, measured at the aptly named Furnace Creek Ranch in Death Valley, California, on July 10, 1913. For decades, the record had been held by El Aziz, Libya, where the mercury supposedly hit 136.4° F in 1922. However, 90 years after that temperature was recorded, meteorologists declared it a false reading by an untrained observer.

DENNIS DEBUNKS:

DENNIS DEBUNKS:
BLACKOUTS LEAD TO BABY BOOMS

Nine months after a blackout (or major blizzard, or volcano eruption, or other stay-in-your-home type disaster) the story is that there will be a baby boom because, really, what else are you going to do if the TV and Internet aren't working? The thing is, the numbers just don't bear this out. Birthrates fluctuate, and believers can always find some event nine months before a baby boom.

185 GET READY TO BLACKOUT

The summer months are sometimes called the "blackout season," as demands on the grid soar and outdated infrastructures overheat and shut down frequently. Here's what to do when the lights go down—and how to prepare before they do.

TURN IT OFF Turn off anything that was on when the blackout began, to avoid taxing the electrical grid when power comes back on. Leave one light or radio on as an indicator for when power is restored. Use an uninterruptible power supply (UPS) for any computers or critical electronics in your home, to give you a way to power your devices even when the power is off and protect against power surges. Use surge protectors (not to be confused with a simple power strip) to protect any electronics not connected to a UPS.

PHONE IT IN If you use cordless phones for your landline, buy a regular corded model that doesn't require power. These usually keep working after the power goes out, and are still the best way to reach emergency services. Keep cash available, either locked in a small safe or hidden away in a lockbox; ATMs and cash registers won't be functional during a blackout.

JUICE UP Stock up on batteries if you are in a blackout-prone area, and consider investing in a solar- or gas-powered generator. When using a generator, be sure to secure it with a cable lock or chain, as it may be sought after by people who don't have one of their own. Have fun while you wait with board games, puzzles, cards, books, and crafts that don't require electricity.

EXTREME WEATHER AROUND THE WORLD:
EUROPEAN HEAT WAVES

Europe is at a pretty high latitude, so it's a quirk of nature that the continent experiences such mild winters. This mild weather is caused by the Gulf Stream, which allows warmer waters from the Gulf of Mexico and the Caribbean to flow northeast toward Europe, where the winds carry sea-warmed air onto the continent. This usually leads to mild summers as well, but the entire continent is highly susceptible to heat waves, during which temperatures in the 90s can kill thousands of people, from Portugal to Poland.

In many regions air conditioning is rare, so people rely on open windows and fans to keep cool in summer. When the air is hot and muggy (even at night), this approach doesn't work. Add in the fact that heat safety isn't widely taught in Europe, and a heat wave can claim a surprising number of lives.

The worst heat wave to strike Europe in modern history unfolded in 2003, when temperatures soared into the 90s and 100s for an entire week, roasting much of western Europe and claiming tens of thousands of lives. Some reports put the death toll as high as 70,000 victims.

186 DREAD THE DERECHO

Heat waves don't just create sweaty, miserable people. Every once in a while—especially in the United States— the formation of a heat wave can lead to a stunning and potentially deadly cluster of thunderstorms that tears across the landscape like a bulldozer. These storms are called mesoscale convective systems (MCS for short).

An MCS is an organized line of thunderstorms that can stretch more than a hundred miles from end to end and screams along a path that ranges thousands of miles in length. Many residents affected by an MCS liken the experience to a hurricane, with a deceptive calm that gives way to ferocious winds and torrential rainfall in a matter of seconds.

Some mesoscale convective systems can develop their own small low-pressure system that creates an astounding swirl on radar imagery—this phenomenon, known as mesoscale convective vortex, can create even stronger straight-line wind gusts and tornadoes, and can even serve as the nucleus for tropical cyclones to develop if the system moves over the ocean.

A particularly powerful MCS is classified as a "derecho," which can cause damage equivalent to that of a weak tornado. An MCS is considered a derecho when it produces significant wind gusts and damage over a continuous path that measures at least 250 miles long.

187 WATCH AN MCS FORM

Mesoscale convective systems often form from clusters of thunderstorms that develop close to one another, such as pop-up thunderstorms or even supercells. If these storms are close enough to each other and in a favorable environment, their cold pools (the rain-cooled air that descends to the surface) can merge together, allowing the thunderstorms to organize into a line.

DEADLY LINEUP This large, unified cold pool can start rolling across the landscape, with thunderstorms following closely behind. The cold pool looks like an invisible bubble, and as it collides with the warm and humid atmosphere in front of it, it forces the unstable air to rise into the storms along its leading edge. This upward motion of unstable air becomes the updraft for the line of storms, allowing them to survive and thrive for as long as the inflow of warm air continues unimpeded.

WICKED WINDS The biggest feature of a mesoscale convective system is the destructive winds it can produce. As the cold pool rushes along the surface, air behind the storms in the pool itself will start rotating vertically, sort of like a wheel rolling across the ground. This rotating air can cause a jet of winds in the mid levels of the atmosphere called a "rear inflow jet"—these winds rush toward the storms from behind, only to collide with the thunderstorms' downdrafts and careen groundward, producing winds at the surface of more than 100 MPH at times.

HOURS OF RAIN Under favorable conditions, a mesoscale convective system can last an impressively long time, surviving for more than a day and traveling thousands of miles from where it began. One of these wind machines won't die out until the cold pool moves too far ahead of the storms to allow air to continue rising, or the line of storms runs into stable air, starving the storms of energy.

188 BRACE FOR A SUPER STORM

The greatest hazard to your safety from an MCS is the destructive winds that form along the storm's leading edge. The wind and rain can hit with little or no warning, a wall of fury that can shear the tops off of trees, topple power lines with ease, and even damage roofs and destroy weak structures like barns and silos before you can tell what hit you.

Aside from the straight-line winds, these lines of storms can produce weak, spin-up tornadoes as they move through an area, exacerbating the damage and creating more opportunities for injury or death for those caught in the path of the storm without proper shelter.

Some of the most dangerous conditions in an MCS are when the systems stall out or move very slowly as they chug along, as they can produce incredible flash flooding. One such situation unfolded in April 2010 along the northern Gulf Coast, when the coastal city of Mobile, Alabama, saw more than 3 inches of rain in just 20 minutes, and some cities in the western Florida Panhandle saw more than 2 feet of rain in one night, leading to catastrophic flash flooding that surpassed the effects of some hurricanes.

The power outages that can result from an MCS—especially a derecho—can be so widespread that hundreds of thousands of people live without power for days on end. Such widespread power outages can cause lingering hazards that surpass the dangers of the storm itself.

189 SURVIVE THE DRY

If you were to picture a desert, you would probably imagine an endless expanse of sand, a couple of cacti, and maybe even a few dangerous critters scurrying about on the ground. Deserts exist all around the world, but our preconceived notions about these arid places are driven by misrepresentations in movies and television shows.

A desert is a dry region of the world where weather and environmental conditions prohibit rainfall through much of the year. Desert locations usually get less than 10 inches of rain per year, but some, like South America's Atacama Desert, can see no rain for decades at a time. It can and does rain in most deserts—just look at cities like Las Vegas and Phoenix—but the entire round of annual rainfall usually occurs over a short wet season.

Along those lines, and contrary to popular belief, not all deserts are hot! The term "desert" refers to the relative lack of precipitation in these regions—while many deserts around the world are blast furnaces, most polar regions see so little precipitation that they can be classified as deserts in their own right. It can also get pretty chilly at night in hot deserts; the same brilliantly clear and sunny sky that allows temperatures to climb to unbearable levels during the day can allow strong radiational cooling to take hold at night, allowing many deserts to experience a large range of temperatures between day and night.

190 FIND THE DESERTS

If you take a look at a satellite image of the Earth, you might notice that most of the deserts around the world are located at roughly the same latitudes. That's no coincidence! Almost all of the world's major deserts have developed around 30°N and 30°S, which are both in the subtropical zones on either side of the equator. As subtropical regions of the world tend to be humid and reliably rainy, you can imagine that it takes some pretty hefty climatic upheavals to create such arid places.

GO WITH THE FLOW One of the major driving factors behind deserts is a large-scale atmospheric circulation known as the Hadley Cell. The circulation begins with rising air near the equator fanning out and flowing toward the poles once it hits the top of the atmosphere above the jet stream. When it reaches about 30°N and 30°S, it sinks toward the ground. This sinking air, known as subsidence, typically produces clear skies and calm conditions. You'll find most famous deserts—the Sahara, the Arabian, the southwestern United States, and the Australian Outback, to name a few—in the regions influenced by Hadley Cell–induced subsidence.

GET SOUTHERN EXPOSURE Among all of the arid regions of the world, there is one that stands out in particular. The Atacama Desert in western South America, around northern Chile, holds the title as the driest place on Earth—some locations can go decades without seeing a single drop of rain. The Atacama is influenced by upwelling in the Pacific Ocean—cold water hitting the side of South America and rising to the surface. This chilly water cools and stabilizes the atmosphere so much that rain and storms hardly ever form over the ocean or over land in this area.

191

FIND WATER IN THE DESERT

Tracking down the rare lush patches that dot an otherwise arid landscape can help lead you to water. It might be below the surface, but it's there, and it's worth digging for.

Scan the distant horizon; if you see a pattern of green, go to it. It might be grasses, or even large trees, fed by an underground spring or puddles remaining from the last rainstorm. Also keep an eye out for dampness near the deepest natural depressions of dry streambeds. If you find moisture, dig, dig, dig. Then place the damp soil in a T-shirt, hold it overhead, and wring it out to release the water.

WEATHER WORLD RECORDS
THE DRIEST PLACE ON EARTH

South America's Atacama Desert is the driest non-polar region on the planet. This 41,000-square-mile strip of land that spans Chile, Peru, Bolivia, and Argentina is composed mainly of salt lakes, sand, and lava. It's estimated that the area may not have had any significant rain between 1570 and 1971. Annual rainfall averages 0.6 inches per year, and some areas go years without any rain at all. In fact, the region is so bleak that it's stood in for Mars in a number of movies.

192

SEEK WATER IN A CANYON

Springs tend to surface at lower levels in canyons, so to find water, start near the canyon mouth and work your way upstream. Moving this way, up-canyon, is safer, as it lessens the chance of your descending a drop-off that you can't climb back up.

In addition to springs, look for "seeps"—moist spots in the canyon floor where water rises up from an underground source. Seeps often result in puddles substantial enough to drink from (although you should, of course, purify the water before doing so).

Beware of both pools and hot springs. Canyon-floor pools can be deceptively cold and deep, and may be difficult to escape from should you fall or jump in. The sulfurous fumes of hot springs can overcome you, and the water can be hot enough to literally boil you alive. Steer clear, no matter how tempting a nice warm wilderness bath might sound.

193 SURVIVE A SANDSTORM

There are some terms in science that appeal to your inner middle-schooler the first time you hear them. "Haboob" is one of them. The term is simply the Arabic word for a sandstorm, or a cloud of sand and dust that can overtake a city and drop visibility to nothing for long periods of time.

STORM CHASERS These impressive and dangerous phenomena are pretty common in and around desert areas, especially during the storm season when gusty winds are likely. Most develop on the edges of storms that sweep through a desert. Strong winds can dig up the loose top layer of sediment from the desert floor, lofting it into the atmosphere and carrying it hundreds or thousands of miles from its original location.

DUST DEVILS Dust storms make daily life extremely difficult; these events are responsible for countless traffic fatalities around the world, not to mention thousands of medical emergencies from dust and sand aggravating respiratory conditions. Some of the largest haboobs on Earth sweep off of the Sahara Desert and into the Atlantic Ocean, sometimes reaching the shores of North America as dust high in the upper atmosphere. This dust is often accompanied by extremely dry air, which can affect weather around the world.

SURVIVAL TIPS Always have goggles and a mask, or at least a bandanna, handy if you're going to be traveling in areas where sandstorms are likely. If you're in a vehicle, and the storm is at a reasonable distance, you may be able to outrun it. Otherwise, stop and ride it out in your car. If you are not in a vehicle and no shelter is near, all you can do is lie down and ride out the storm. Get to higher ground, if possible. The blowing sand is most concentrated close to the ground. Cover your head with your arms or a backpack to protect against any objects being hurled by the wind.

FALL

This season is a transition for millions of schoolchildren every year and, in the meteorological world, fall is also more of a transition than anything else. It's a stepping stone, a halfway point, the boring journey to the cruel, unrelenting destination that is winter. The other transition season—spring—is defined by thunderstorms and tornadoes. During an average spring day, we either revel in the world around us or run for our lives. Spring has some personality, while fall is just three seasons masquerading as one.

Autumn has a little bit of everything all wrapped up in one quick quarter of the year—summer heat, winter cold, hurricanes, tornadoes, snow. You never really know what you're going to get, and these wild shifts in weather all depend on where you live. For most of the world's population in the mid latitudes, the first half of fall is just summer winding down, while the second half of fall is pretty much winter lite.

Even though spring is a more exciting transition than fall, there are some hazards you need to keep in mind while you take in the beauty of the decaying world around you. The switch from summer to fall can bring about destructive wildfires that can destroy millions of acres of land with little effort. A select set of unlucky communities have to stand guard against an incredible phenomenon known as lake-effect snow. Vast weather patterns around the world can shift when the waters in certain parts of the Pacific Ocean grow warmer or colder than normal, presenting as events known as El Niño and La Niña.

Fall is a little boring and hard to define—oddly, that's what makes it interesting.

194

DEAL WITH A DROUGHT

Drought is simply an absence of moisture, when below-average rainfall depletes water stores and dries up wells. There's no specific moment at which a dry spell becomes a drought. Some droughts have been declared after just a couple of weeks. What matters most is how long droughts last. In normal circumstances, a drought can last for a few months to a year. But more extreme droughts, such as the one in California, that began in 2012 can last years before the cycle is broken.

HAVE A PLAN Developed countries are typically sheltered from the deleterious effects of droughts, notably loss of food and drinking water. These countries typically have reserves and food options available that render the drought's effects moot unless you live or work in an industry that is water dependent. Farmers and ranchers have to plan ahead in ways average citizens do not. Similarly, city governments and municipalities have to have a water-conservation plan, which may include taking water-intensive farmlands out of rotation to keep the water for residents.

SEE IT COMING The key to drought management is recognizing the conditions in their early stages. While droughts can't be effectively predicted yet, historical data illustrates that they will happen and happen often. As a result, governments monitor not only rainfall but also peripheral conditions like snowpack, water tables, reservoir levels, and humidity trends. Additional factors like extended periods of high heat or wind also can exacerbate the conditions that lead to a drought. Monitoring all these factors helps governments recognize droughts and act accordingly.

195 DROUGHT-PROOF YOUR HOME

Water conservation isn't very sexy. And in places like the United States, where quality water comes on demand from the tap, most people are cavalier about their water consumption. However, we have a history of damaging the environment and causing disasters. Look no further than the Dust Bowl of the 1930s for an example of how effectively we can screw things up. To get a jump on conservation, just look at the measures imposed during drought conditions. All you have to do is be proactive.

LOOK TO YOUR LAWN Everyone hates mowing, so go for a longer, lusher lawn. Tall grass is more efficient and loses less water in drought conditions. Likewise, give your sprinklers a tune-up, fixing clogs and leaks. Then give the sprinkler a break. Water less frequently, and at times when evaporation is less likely. Go a step further by installing an automated sprinkler system that monitors moisture content and waters only when needed, to avoid over-watering.

COLLECT RAIN Even in droughts, it still rains. A rain catchment system can help hold that water for lawns and gardens, putting less stress on municipal water supplies.

PLANT SMART Many homeowners in drought-stricken California have started replacing their lawns with fake turf. If you aren't willing to go that far, try installing a rock garden with fewer, drought-tolerant plants. You also can group plants together in any yard by their watering needs, which should help to reduce over-watering. Or look into drip irrigation systems.

DON'T FLUSH (As often.) Inside your home, flushing is the second biggest water waster. Toilets account for nearly 20% of a home's water usage. Check for leaks and fix them. Even better, upgrade to a new, low-flow toilet. If you're ambitious, you can install a composting toilet.

SKIP THE RINSE Clean laundry is a necessity, but check the washer settings. Skip the second rinse cycle, and wash your clothes on a smaller load setting. A plumber also can reroute your gray water to trees and gardens rather than into a sewer.

WASH LIKE A SAILOR Finally, clean yourself smarter. To preserve water on Navy ships, sailors hop in the shower, get wet, then turn off the water to wash. They turn the water back on for rinsing. You'll be surprised at how much water you save by doing the same. Likewise, turn off the water while brushing your teeth.

EXTREME WEATHER HISTORY:
THE AMERICAN DUST BOWL

Many factors contributed to the devastation of the Dust Bowl, including drought conditions, more efficient mechanized farm equipment like small gas tractors, and a lack of understanding about how much damage human activity could do. For much of the "Dirty Thirties," farmlands in the Great Plains of the United States and Canada quite literally blew away in huge clouds of dust that often darkened the sky. These dust clouds earned the moniker "Black Blizzard," and some reached as far as New York on the East Coast.

Many parts of America's grain belt receive as little as 10 inches of rain a year, but the tall prairie grasses helped trap moisture in the soil, even during drought conditions. Then farmers small and large eschewed dry-farming techniques, instead opting for deep plowing and furrows. Come harvest time, combine tractors stripped away the plants necessary to keep the soil intact. The result, in hindsight, was predictable. The virgin topsoil quickly turned to dust. And that dust, in turn, was picked up and carried away by the wind.

More than 100 million acres of land were impacted by the event, with Texas and Oklahoma the hardest hit. At least 10,000 families were displaced by the Dust Bowl, with most heading to California in the hopes of finding a better livelihood. However, the Great Depression made life there and in other states little better than it was back in Oklahoma. Many banks in the plains states also folded during this time, making scarce the credit that might have helped farmers.

In the areas most widely impacted, as much as 75% of fertile topsoil was lost in the massive dust storms. Still, it took nearly two decades before government incentives designed to conserve soil and new farming techniques were embraced. However, as a result of this ecological disaster, progressive farming did emerge, with crop rotations and a shift away from monoculture to more diverse crop plantings. In many locations, grain crops were replaced with hay production and animal ranching.

196 HUNT THE DROUGHT

In drought years, deer populations decrease while the number of harvested deer likely increases. The reason is simple. Female deer are less likely to care for fawns birthed in drought conditions. But, at the same time, deer that are stressed for food will alter their feeding habits and head toward areas where food is more plentiful, such as farms (where crops are grown) and ranches (where animals are fed grains or pellets).

WATCH ANIMAL BEHAVIOR Many animals behave differently than they might during normal weather conditions. With water at a premium, both prey and predators begin congregating where water is available, and predators may be emboldened as competition increases. Also, vegetation is impacted, leading animals like deer to revert to eating habits normally only seen in winter conditions, such as eating bark and less-nutritious leaves from older plants and trees.

FOLLOW THE FOOD Whitetail hunters, in particular, might consider changing their tactics during a prolonged drought. With deer moving into areas where food is more available, hunters may find farmers and ranchers more receptive to hunting on their properties in order to help control the deer population.

HUNT CONSERVATIVELY Bucks may be more plentiful in these times, but hunters may find that their antlers are smaller, as the poor nutrition impacts growth. The emphasis for the dry-season hunter should be on filling the freezer with meat rather than getting a trophy buck. Adult deer naturally take care of themselves to breed in better years. Hunters can help alleviate the stress by harvesting smaller bucks who may not be dominant, and by taking older does (if they take a doe at all). Smart hunting can help the deer population bounce back faster from harsh drought conditions.

197 FISH THE DROUGHT

If wildfire is a necessary vehicle for forest renewal, drought can have the same impact on fisheries. While fishing might be a more challenging endeavor during a drought, there still are some positive effects of lower water levels. There are some issues, though, that anglers may not expect. In drought-stressed areas, fishing licenses sometimes are less available. With a potential loss of spawning grounds for lake fish, for example, too many people fishing a stressed population can decimate it. Some common sense helps recognize both the good and the bad results of a drought on fishing.

THE GOOD

Less pressure means more fish have a chance to survive to a larger size. Some of the best fishing you'll experience will be in the year after a drought.

Lower water levels can make it easier to repair docks and piers that might otherwise be neglected. Likewise, boat owners can take the opportunity to make repairs or perform maintenance.

Bait fish will concentrate rather than spreading out over a broader area, meaning it will be easier for larger, predatory fish to thin them out.

Fishing lower water levels allows fishermen to work structures and hidden cover that might otherwise be out of reach.

Governments and volunteer organizations often use this time to complete habitat renewal projects.

THE BAD

Lower water levels can lead to more obstacles in the boating lanes, so keep a sharp eye out.

Fewer fishing licenses may be issued, and limits may be reduced or altered.

Bank fishing may be out of the question as waters recede.

Marinas and bait shops will feel the pinch from fewer people fishing.

A loss of spawning areas may impact adult fish populations years later.

198 CATCH YOUR RAIN

A lot of people hear "rain catchment" and think of a system that is either too large to be practical, or too complicated to DIY. Here's a quick and easy way to grab the rain. It's an afternoon project that can have a huge impact in a drought. Do note that you'll have even more success with this system if you have a roofline within a gutter. Also, make sure it's legal in your area.

STEP 1 Make a trough by screwing three deck boards together—one as the base, and two as the sides. Use a clear, silicone sealer along the seams to keep the water from leaking out. When choosing your wood, avoid synthetics and pressure-treated lumber.

STEP 2 Buy a handful of containers (the number will depend on the size of your rain trough) suitable for storing water. Choose containers that have a 2-inch opening.

STEP 3 Line up your containers under the trough. Remember that containers expand when filled, so leave a little space between them. Then use a hole saw attached to a power drill to cut holes in the bottom of the trough.

STEP 4 Cut 6-inch lengths of PVC pipe that fit in the holes in the bottom of your trough. Then use PVC narrowing conduits at the top of each length. Use a miter saw to cut out a small area of the conduit where it sits on the trough. This cutout will help funnel water directly into your containers. You also can drill several holes of substantial diameter to achieve the same end.

STEP 5 Drop the pipe/conduit into the trough cutouts and into the container openings. More silicone sealer around the base will help keep you from losing water.

Once you've got your system set up, you can fashion some simple legs to attach to the end. Then just set up your trough and wait for it to rain.

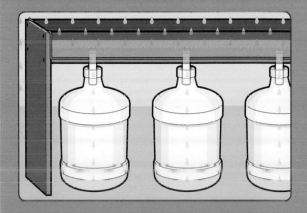

199 LET IT BURN (SAFELY)

The very element that sparked the advancement and survival of humankind is able to take it away in one swift instant. Fire is a terrifying and powerful force that shows no mercy to anything in its path. Much safety education around the world is devoted to preventing and dealing with the scourge of fire. The majority of blazes that occur in our homes and vehicles are easily preventable, but the flames that can reduce miles of land to ash aren't always so easy to stop.

Wildfires can burn a small patch of grass or huge expanses of forest, eliminating hundreds of years of growth and clouding the sky with so much billowing smoke that people thousands of miles away are affected by the burned remains of another continent's former beauty.

Some fires are more dangerous than others—most burn harmlessly out in the middle of nowhere, threatening few or no humans in the process, while a few can threaten heavily populated cities or produce choking, toxic smoke that can injure or kill people thousands of miles away.

Fires are nature's way of cleaning up the place—almost all of the fires that occur in the wild are sparked by lightning, burning the dead matter and underbrush that crowds the ground and stifles new growth. Wildfires are a natural and healthy part of the environment's life cycle, but as humanity grew and expanded into previously uninhabited lands, even small blazes became a life-threatening nuisance.

It contradicts everything we were taught as children, but those fire-safety messages from the likes of that preachy, anthropomorphic bear have been too effective—we're so good at preventing even small fires that forests and wooded areas are wildly overgrown, so much so that tiny fires can blow up into monsters that engulf huge expanses of real estate and threaten more people than they would have otherwise.

One of the best ways we can recognize the hazards of wildfires and survive them in the future is to realize that we need to let some fires burn. Some buildings and habitats will be destroyed in the process, but it's a natural part of the environment, and disrupting the trend would prove more disastrous and deadly in the long run.

200 PREDICT A FIRE

Meteorologists can use forecast models and observations to predict when the right combination of heat, humidity, wind, and other variables like vegetation moisture will create dangerous fire weather in any particular location. The U.S. National Weather Service issues red flag warnings when weather conditions could lead to the rapid formation and spread of fires. Here are the four major conditions that can prime an environment to go up in smoke.

HEAT It seems like heat would be the most important variable, but all heat does is allow the relative humidity to drop dangerously low. Hot summer days in a dry atmosphere can drive relative humidity down to 10% or even lower, allowing vegetation to dry up like jerky and give fires the fuel they need to rage.

HUMIDITY Relative humidity is "relative" because it measures the amount of moisture in the air when you take into account both dew point and air temperature. When they're close together, relative humidity is high, and when they're far apart, there's very low relative humidity. We've all experienced those days when our skin dries out in an instant—just imagine what those extremely low humidity levels do to plants. Days with low relative humidity can easily suck the moisture out of vegetation, making it an easy target for fire to consume.

WIND The wind plays a critical role in whether or not a fire remains localized or spreads into an epic inferno. Winds as low as 15 MPH are sufficient to transport sparks to surrounding fuel, allowing something as small as a campfire to spread to neighboring trees, turning into a blaze that firefighters can struggle for weeks to control.

STORMS Not all thunderstorms are accompanied by precipitation. Many drier climates are plagued by a phenomenon known as "dry thunderstorms" during the warm season. These storms produce little or no precipitation, allowing lightning to strike dried-out vegetation with no rain to extinguish the flames. Lightning produced by dry thunderstorms is responsible for some of the worst fires in the western United States.

EXTREME WEATHER AROUND THE WORLD: SOUTHERN CALIFORNIA

California is regularly affected by severe drought conditions. Droughts don't necessarily cause wildfires, but they do exacerbate the conditions. There aren't many plants that can survive a sustained drought, so exceptionally dry conditions that last for a long period of time wreak havoc on regional flora, leaving millions of acres of land exposed to disaster if one errant spark lands in the wrong spot at the wrong time.

California has to deal with this all the time, and there are local conditions that can make the situation even worse. Southern California is especially vulnerable to destructive wildfires due to a phenomenon known as the Santa Ana winds. These winds typically occur during the fall when a high pressure system sets up over Arizona or Nevada. The clockwise winds blow up and over the mountains, warming up and drying out as they race down toward the coast. These dry winds can blow at over 70 MPH in the most extreme cases, allowing raging wildfires to threaten millions of people.

202
DON'T TRUST THE COLD

Imagine that it's the end of September and you're enjoying a warm fall day at your home in Minnesota. A dry cold front passed through the area a few hours ago, bringing a couple of clouds, but none of the rain that typically comes with storm systems that swing through the area. Even though the feature was a cold front, it acted more like a dry line you'd see in Oklahoma—dew points dropped significantly, but temperatures didn't budge too much.

The combination of gusty winds behind the front, warm temperatures, and low relative humidity levels all primed the environment for brushfires across the region. By nightfall, hundreds of acres of countryside burn as a result of homeowners burning leaves, running gas-powered equipment in brush, or flicking cigarettes out the car window, despite a red flag warning that implores citizens to refrain from these careless activities.

This scenario isn't that far-fetched—situations like the one above occur frequently in locations where warmer temperatures, low humidity, and breezy conditions come together just right to allow fires to form. It doesn't feel like you're sitting in a tinderbox in western Colorado, but the silent danger exists just the same.

201
RIDE OUT AN INFERNO

When a fire is approaching, the smart thing to do is leave. Early. The number one cause of death in wildfires is evacuating too late. When firefighters issue an evacuation order, you should go. But let's say, for some reason, you didn't leave. You didn't get out in time, and now the road is covered in smoke, power lines are down, and the road is covered with embers. You can't just hop in the car and drive away now. So what do you do?

Terrifyingly, ou stay inside. Radiant heat is the biggest concern during a raging wildfire. So simply put, the house is the safest place to be. The risk, obviously, is your house going up in flames, too. Make certain you take fire safety seriously, and firescape your home before you have to. You can't clear brush from around your home when it's already burning. The second leading cause of death in wildfires? People outside the home trying to defend it from every ember. Getting into a running shower may give you some protection.

Assuming you've survived, the real time to be outside defending your home, surprisingly enough, is after the fire has passed. Many homes catch fire from residual embers in clogged gutters, wood piles, leaf litter, and the like. These areas absolutely can be taken care of, sometimes with a simple bucket of water. Plan ahead, though. You need to have a pump and water to protect your home, and those might not be available in an emergency situation.

WEATHER WORLD RECORDS
MOST DESTRUCTIVE WILD FIRE

While different fires might claim this unenviable title depending on area burned, lives lost, or dollars in damage, there's little argument that Australia's Black Saturday bushfires in 2009 stand among the worst. Following a terrible drought, more than 400 fires joined to devastate over a million acres, killing 173 people and injuring at least 414.

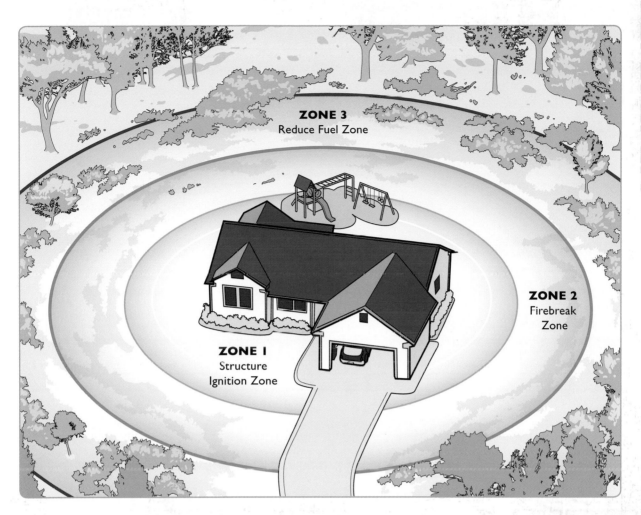

ZONE 3
Reduce Fuel Zone

ZONE 2
Firebreak
Zone

ZONE 1
Structure
Ignition Zone

203 FIRESCAPE YOUR HOME

Homeowners in fire-prone areas have long understood that prevention really does go a long way. But you can use these tips in any area, even in cities, to help keep your home safe. Clearing the area around your home can make the difference between simply surviving a wildfire, and surviving it with a home to return to.

On your house itself, keep 1/8" mesh over all vent coverings to prevent embers from entering the attic or other spaces. And be sure to use fire-retardant tiles and materials where possible on the roof and other walls. Try dividing your property into four zones, then prepare each zone accordingly. None of this is a guarantee that your home will make it through unscathed, but it can tip the odds in your favor.

ZONE 1 Mark out an area 30 feet around your home. This is the critical zone. Don't allow any tall plants or trees in this area. Instead, if you keep a lawn, keep it low, well-irrigated, and green. Resist those pretty bushes and tall flowers up against your house. Instead, keep it open. Even in the city, this space will allow fire vehicles access to any location they need to reach.

ZONE 2 Within that 30-foot buffer, but away from the house, go with drought-tolerant plants. A drip irrigation system in this zone also will keep the soil moist and the plants healthy and less prone to fire damage.

ZONE 3 In choosing to plant trees (or to leave trees standing), think about height. Pick species that are a little lower, underneath that 30-foot height, so if they fall, they won't fall on any structures. Low-growing, drought-resistant plants here also function as better ground cover. If the low vegetation catches fire, you want to keep upward and outward sparks at a minimum. Do not plant conifers—they can virtually explode in high heat.

ZONE 4 This is the safe zone farthest away from your house. Don't allow your home to transition straight from manicured to wild, however. You don't have to do a ton of work here, but keep the ground cover knocked down, and clear out any dead vegetation.

204 RECOGNIZE A FIRE WHIRL

When a fire reaches the point that it is creating its own wind, a possible outcome is a fire whirl. Mostly, fire whirls are just cool to look at, but they can be a serious issue. Temperatures in the core of a fire whirl can reach 2,000 degrees Fahrenheit, which is hot enough to reignite ash and burned debris sucked into it. The vortex can then send these embers in new directions, igniting structures and unburned areas.

If you really want to freak yourself out, a 2013 report verified that an EF-2 tornado in Australia was spawned from Pyrocumulonimbus clouds and the winds from a wildfire. That's right. A fire's winds were strong enough to create a supercell thunderstorm, which then spawned an EF-2 tornado inside the wildfire that created it. The fire whirl was 500 meters in diameter.

The most extreme examples of fire whirls are from history. During the 1923 Kanto Earthquake, a firestorm erupted, spawning a massive fire whirl that killed 38,000 people in just 15 minutes. Similarly, in 1926 in San Luis Obispo, California, lightning strikes caused a four-day conflagration at an oil storage facility. Numerous whirls resulted from the fire, causing structural damage in areas well away from the center. These whirls were responsible for killing two and hurling burning embers and debris as far as 3 miles away.

205 SURVIVE A WILDFIRE

You're out on a hike or a hunt or just a stroll, and the next thing you know, you're running for your life from a wildfire. What do you do to survive? I'm not going to lie. Surviving a wildfire is tough, but there are some tactics to try.

GET OUT A lot of people want to wait around to see how things develop. But wildfires can chew up land at 70 MPH. By the time you realize you're in immediate danger, it's often too late.

KNOW THE AREA If you're out someplace you've never been, maintain situational awareness at all times. And have a plan of escape.

GET DOWNHILL Fire moves fastest uphill. That's bad news, because people move slowest when running uphill. Avoid draws and canyons; look for the escape that leads to open, lower elevation.

DROP YOUR GEAR Get yourself out. Trying to run with gear or staying around too long trying to pack things up will only slow you down.

GET LOW If the fire has caught up to you, look for the lowest point you can find and get into it. Think ditch, culvert, or wash out.

USE YOUR CLOTHES If you have a canteen, wet your shirt and cover your face with it. Breathing through it will help you avoid smoke inhalation.

CLEAR A SPACE If you come across an open area that's already burned and free of fuel, riding out the fire there might be your best bet. Be prepared—it's going to be an oven. Radiant temperatures are deadly, even in a blackened area. Don't try burning out a space on your own. You'll likely just start the fire that kills you.

SHELTER IN PLACE And by shelter, we're talking about a fire shelter. These are small, lightweight tents that can reflect as much as 95% of a fire's radiant heat. Make sure you're clear of any snags or overhangs that can fall on you, pop open the shelter, and pray.

EXTREME WEATHER HISTORY:
2010 RUSSIAN WILDFIRES

Russia is the largest country in the world, stretching across nine time zones and sitting on a solid 11% of the world's total land. A country that large experiences the whole spectrum of weather conditions, from roaring thunderstorms to brutal blizzards, and just about everything in between. It's no surprise that such a large, sparsely populated country is vulnerable to some of the worst wildfires in recent history.

The summer of 2010 was a historic season for Russia, clocking in as the country's all-time hottest summer ever recorded. Temperatures frequently cracked the 90s and 100s in cities across the western and central part of the country, creating dire conditions for vulnerable residents, especially those without the supplies or means to cool themselves off. In this case, however, Russians didn't only have the heat to worry about, but also the choking smoke that blanketed the region for weeks on end.

A persistent upper-level ridge in the jet stream and high pressure at the surface allowed hot temperatures, low humidity, and breezy conditions to prevail across vast expanses of the forested country, permitting wildfires to spring up and burn millions of acres of land over the course of two months. Not only did weather conditions exacerbate the blazes, but the remoteness of the fires made it hard or impossible for crews to fight the flames, allowing the fires to burn out of control until they ran out of fuel or weather conditions improved.

The flames caused billions of dollars in damage, claiming dozens of lives and indirectly causing an unknown number of additional casualties from the extreme air pollution that swept over millions during the worst of the fires. Smoke from the fires was so intense that many locations in North America, thousands of miles to the east, reported seeing thick smoke and haze during the event.

DENNIS DEBUNKS:
LA NIÑA ALWAYS FOLLOWS EL NIÑO

If you live somewhere that's currently being affected by an El Niño, you've no doubt heard everyone from your grandma to the milkman saying, "Well, this'll be followed by La Niña next year, so it'll all even out." In fact, while this pattern does seem to happen more often than chance would dictate, it's by no means a foregone conclusion.

206 MEET THE KIDS

Major shifts in weather patterns can thrust formerly obscure terms to the forefront of the public's mind; the polar vortex, for example, has been around forever and was discovered in the 1800s, but everyone freaked out when they heard about it for the first time in January 2014. Similar hype has occurred with other common weather patterns as well, and El Niño is one of them.

El Niño is one of the most widely known weather phenomena, in large part thanks to a series of natural disasters that occurred in the U.S. during the 1980s and 1990s as a result of this oceanic warming in the Pacific.

Fishermen off the northwestern coast of South America were among the first to notice the effects of El Niño, when warmer-than-normal temperatures led to an explosion in sea creature populations in the region. The term "El Niño" translates to "the little boy" in Spanish, which is a reference to the baby Jesus, since these fishermen first discovered the phenomenon during the Christmas season.

Now, how does the water warm up? Well, through processes that scientists are still working to better understand, trade winds over the equatorial Pacific can calm down or even reverse toward the east, pushing warm water off the coast of Australia and Oceania east toward South America. This warm water overpowers upwelling—cold water that rises to the surface from deep in the ocean—and causes water temperatures to climb above normal near Peru and Ecuador.

When the opposite effect was described, it just made sense to call it "La Niña," or "the little girl."

El Niño and La Niña are part of a larger system called the "El Niño Southern Oscillation," or ENSO for short. ENSO deals with the large-scale shift of weather patterns and currents in the Pacific Ocean, which are responsible for altering weather conditions around the world. El Niño is defined as when sea surface temperatures in the eastern Pacific Ocean are 0.5°C above normal for three consecutive months. A La Niña is when they drop to 0.5°C below normal.

El Niños and La Niñas both occur every three to five years on average, although it can be as short as two or as long as seven years between events. They can last anywhere from a few months to two years, although nine to 12 months is standard. It's estimated that over the past 50 years, about 31% of the time El Niño conditions have prevailed, 23% of the time was La Niña, and the rest "normal." El Niño gets a lot more press because it was discovered first, and had a major impact on the region where it was first described, while La Niña's effects were relatively minor. Once we realized that it was a global pattern, however, it's become clear that both can herald devastating and dangerous conditions.

207 GO WITH THE FLOW

The equatorial Pacific Ocean stretches from Australia and Oceania east to South America—a vast expanse of ocean, where even small variations in sea surface temperatures can have major consequences for global weather. Knowing these conditions and their effects can help you guess what's coming, and be able to prepare. The complexity of the system means we need to say things like "It's usually the case that" or "has a tendency to." Weather is really, really complicated. That said, here's what you might expect around the world.

	EL NIÑO	LA NINA
GENERAL CONDITIONS	Trade winds over the equatorial Pacific calm down or even reverse toward the east, pushing warm water off the coast of Australia and Oceania east toward South America. The warm water overpowers upwelling—cold water that rises to the surface from deep in the ocean—and causes water temperatures to climb above normal near Peru and Ecuador.	Strong trade winds blow from the east, causing abnormally warm waters to pool in the western equatorial Pacific near Australia and allowing upwelling to take hold in the east near South America, forcing sea surface temperatures to cool below normal. Sea level can rise by almost a foot in the western half of the ocean.
PRECIPITATION	• Warmer temperatures in the eastern Pacific create warmer and more unstable air, leading to an explosion in thunderstorm activity. • Higher than normal precipitation across equatorial regions. Major flooding, particularly in Peru and Ecuador, from April through October. • In North America, much of the northwest experiences a warmer, drier winter; the southern and eastern states have a cooler, wetter season. • Europe experiences a colder, drier winter in the north, and a warmer, wetter one in the south.	• Heavy rains in Southeast Asia and Oceania. Higher than normal rainfall and catastrophic flooding in the Andes. • In the U.S., above-average rainfall in the Midwest, Rockies, and Pacific Northwest, and below-average rainfall in the southeastern and southwestern states. • Colder, snowier winter in Canada
TROPICAL STORMS	• Upper-level wind shear can flow into the Atlantic and kill hurricanes before they form and move north. • Decreased wind shear to the east increases cyclone activity in the eastern Pacific, but these storms rarely make landfall.	• Lack of thunderstorm activity in the summer can allow an above-normal number of tropical cyclones to form in the Atlantic Basin.
DROUGHT	• Can lead to extreme drought conditions over Australia and the islands that make up Oceania. • Exacerbates drought conditions in California. • Can cause drought and famine in West Africa.	• Drought can devastate the coastal regions of Peru and Chile. • Exacerbates drought conditions in the American Southwest.

208 DON'T FALL FOR IT

Have you ever gone to bed after a long day and heard a noise just as you're starting to fall asleep? "It was nothing," you think. "It's just the ice maker clicking on." But then some other thoughts invade your resting mind. "What if it was a burglar? Did the dog see a ghost? Where is the dog, anyway? Did I lock the door? Did I forget to shut off the stove?" Your imagination begins to run wild and you have to get out of bed to make sure everything is okay.

This thought process can manifest itself on a grand scale, known as a conspiracy theory. Conspiracy theories assert that a group of people are responsible for a vast cover-up that conceals the truth about some major event, such as a political assassination or even the cause or purpose of a war.

Conspiracy theories allow us to take real-world events and turn them into fictions that live within our minds (and on the websites we create about them). These tall tales have taken root in society for as long as there's been society, but they're able to grow and live forever in the modern Internet age.

In most cases, things really are as they seem at a cursory glance. Sometimes people get shot. Sometimes hurricanes hit just the right area to cause major death and destruction. It's when people don't like or accept the facts of a situation that they start to make up stories, seeing shadows on the wall that really aren't there. Most of the time, that click in the night really is just the ice maker, and not some squad of Russian commandos invading your home to hold you hostage for all the nukes in the world.

The vast majority of conspiracy theories are harmless. After all, there are people who believe that the moon is a projected hologram in the sky and that Elvis is still alive and running a gas station in Idaho. Sure, whatever! But some can actually be dangerous, including some odd beliefs about the weather.

209 KNOW WHO'S CONTROLLING THE WEATHER

Humans have wanted to control the weather for as long as we've existed, for good reason. If we could pull it off, droughts would be eliminated, crops would flourish, disasters would all but disappear. It would eliminate the need for meteorologists, and it could give rise to a supercharged level of global politics that could devolve into a world war. Just who gets to control the weather? Who determines where rain falls? What if rain that's sufficient for one crop kills another?

That's all a matter of science fiction, of course. The atmosphere is so large and complex that it would be impossible to control it to satisfy our whims and needs. There are a couple of things we can do on a limited scale (intentionally or not) to alter the way the atmosphere works, but nobody is able to control the weather like an evil movie villain.

There's a small subset of the population, though, that fervently believes that a secret world government is using various technologies to control the weather and develop disasters from thin air. (These puppet masters apparently really have it in for trailer parks.)

The only form of weather modification that's been successful at all to date is something called "cloud seeding." The idea behind it is that you can seed preexisting clouds with fine particulates to act as nuclei, collecting water droplets from the cloud and forcing rain to fall. Research indicates that it can work over small areas under the right conditions, but it's not viable as a drought reliever because first of all, you need to have enough clouds for it to work and, even if you do, the rain falls over a limited area for a limited amount of time. Sorry, Dr. Evil.

210 WATCH THE SKIES

Tens of thousands of airplanes take flight every day around the world, transporting millions of passengers all over the globe. Some of these planes fly so high that the only way we can see them at all is by the clouds they leave in their wake. We're all familiar with the long, white streaks that frequently form behind high-flying airplanes. These wispy clouds are called condensation trails, or contrails for short.

Contrails form when the warm, moist exhaust from airplane engines condenses in the cold, moist air in the upper atmosphere, much like the process that lets you see your breath on a winter's morning. Some days they only last a couple of minutes, while on other days the skies can be filled with dozens of these trails, spreading out in a translucent haze. Contrails are made up of condensed water vapor and other pollutants that result from the burning of jet fuel—that is to say, they're mostly harmless except for that whole "polluting the environment" thing.

Beginning in the 1990s, a small but vocal group of people started asserting that these condensation trails were really "chemtrails," or trails of chemicals sprayed by airplanes to control the weather (or for various other nefarious purposes).

Even leaving aside the difficulty of maintaining a global conspiracy with millions of participants sworn to secrecy, there are a few other tiny problems with the theory, including the enormous cost of such an operation, and the fact that it's physically impossible when you calculate the number of airplanes and the weight of the chemicals required. Plus, apparently the government in this theory is really bad at chemtrailing, since the weather doesn't seem to have miraculously started favoring any one nation.

This seems like a harmless obsession, but some unhinged theorists have even gone so far as to threaten to shoot down aircraft they suspect of spraying these nonexistent chemicals. This is a prime example of how a simple, seemingly harmless conspiracy theory can pose a real threat to the public.

211 WATCH THAT VOLCANO

It's bad enough that we have to worry about the weather trying to kill us, but we also have to worry about other disasters that cause crazy weather. For example, a volcano can blow you up, suffocate you, or incinerate you if you're too close when it erupts. But even if you live thousands of miles away, it can still mess with you. The fact is, volcanoes can alter global weather patterns and impact climate years after an eruption.

The most obvious effect on global weather of a catastrophic volcanic eruption would be a thick layer of volcanic ash, dust, and debris that would remain suspended in the atmosphere, much as we would see after a meteor or comet strike. This persistent layer of junk in the atmosphere would reflect sunlight and lower temperatures by several degrees, which doesn't sound like much, but it's a major climactic shift and we'd need to adjust.

One of the most violent volcanic eruptions on record occurred in 1883, when Indonesia's Krakatoa erupted with a bang that remains unrivaled today. The shock wave from the blast circled the world several times, showing up on monitoring devices for days after the explosion. The eruption darkened the sky worldwide for years afterward.

In addition, the sulfuric gas ejected by the volcano caused clouds to reflect sunlight away from the earth, lowering the world's temperatures for the next five years. Record amounts of rain fell around the globe, some of it acid rain due to the sulfur. Indonesia has a wealth of other potentially deadly volcanos, but if you want something really terrifying to fixate on, read up on the supervolcano in Yellowstone Park.

The upside? Shutter bugs would love the spectacular sunrises and sunsets. Volcanic ash is able to effectively scatter reds and oranges in the atmosphere, allowing vivid sunsets one would normally only see in manipulated photographs or paintings. In fact, it's theorized that the blood-red sky that appears in the famous painting "The Scream" is an accurate depiction of the color of the sky over Norway at the time it was painted, shortly after Krakatoa's eruption.

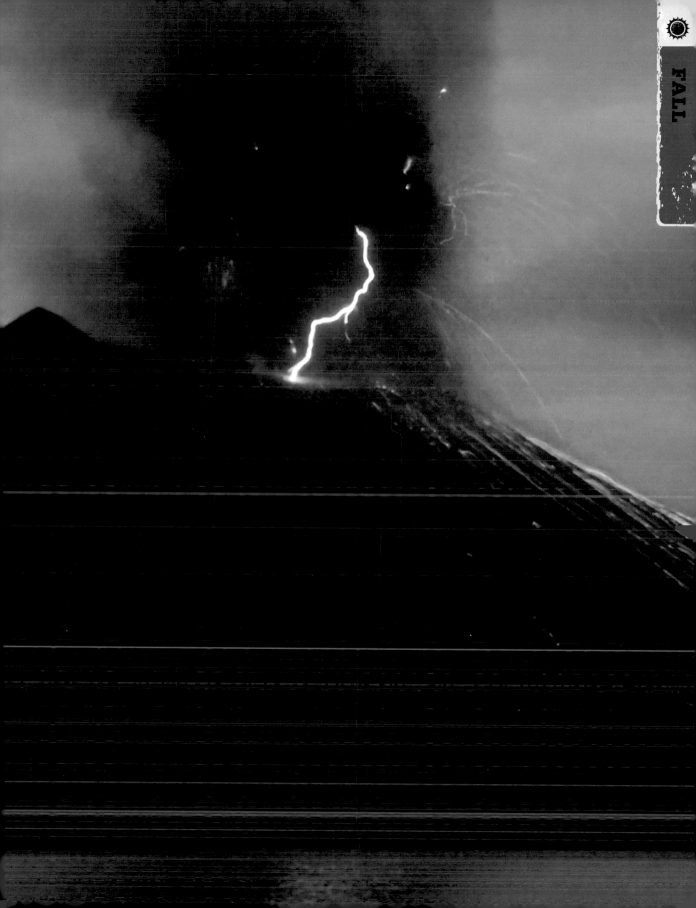

212 PREPARE FOR THE END OF THE WORLD AS WE KNOW IT

It's quite clear that weather can kill any of us. And that it can, in catastrophic cases, kill hundreds, even thousands of people. But can bad weather kill everybody? Depending on what caused that weather, the answer is probably yes.

Some cataclysmic event like a meteor or comet striking the Earth would have dramatic consequences on global weather, and it's hard to think of a scenario in which most people who lived through the disaster would survive very long. The dinosaurs were much tougher and angrier than we are, and look at how well they fared when the comet struck.

Let's say a rather large meteor careens through the atmosphere and strikes the ocean. Assuming that you survive the ensuing tsunamis, earthquakes, and initial rain of debris, the future still looks pretty bleak. Hurricane activity would cease due to a lack of the heat necessary to warm ocean waters, which doesn't sound so bad—except for the fact that nothing else would be warm either. Fine particles would remain suspended in the atmosphere for months and years after impact, obscuring the sun to the point that plant life would die out within months. The lack of sunlight would also steadily plunge temperatures, leading to cold days and frigid nights around the world. Once plants and animals die off, even resourceful humans would run out of food.

In other words, the change in weather after a meteor impact would ensure that not only humans, but most life on Earth would come to a swift, grim demise. Sleep tight!

213 BEAM ME UP

Speaking of theories that could come straight from the mind of a comic book villain, imagine a device that shoots high-energy beams into the atmosphere in order to create enormous tornadoes that wipe out entire towns thousands of miles away. Outlandish, right? Well, there are people who believe in this, too.

Like a lot of wacky ideas, it has a tiny kernel of truth at its center. Or, in a remote part of southern Alaska in this case. That's where a government project known as the High Frequency Active Auroral Research Program, or HAARP, was located from 1993 until it was permanently closed in 2014. The station housed a gridded array of antennas that emitted high-frequency radio waves into the ionosphere in order to study how this region at the top of the atmosphere affects radio communications.

That's kind of boring. Wouldn't it be much cooler if those high-energy waves were really used to trigger disasters around the world, including spawning tornadoes and spinning up hurricanes? Because it just makes sense that the evil masterminds would be messing with people who live in trailer parks instead of overthrowing the government. Jerks.

(Also, despite the best efforts of evil masterminds the world over, we haven't quite figured out how to use radio waves to control the weather. Yet.)

214 SURVIVE THE COLD WAR

During the stressful days of the Cold War, one of the many terrifying consequences of all-out nuclear war was the prospect of something called a "nuclear winter." The concept stems from the idea that one country nuking another would lead to multiple countries lobbing nuclear bombs at each other until everyone and everything was destroyed, including the global climate. Assuming some portion of the world lived through this deadly, radioactive temper tantrum, the resulting change in weather could throw a wrench in humanity's continued survival.

The driving force behind the so-called nuclear winter is the same as what would cause global temperatures to dip after a strike by a space rock or a major volcanic eruption—essentially, air pollution. Really, really bad air pollution. The theory is that the bombs would cause fires, which in turn would burn cities and forests, releasing vast amounts of smoke, ash, soot, dust, and dirt into the atmosphere, where it would stay for years. The particles would prevent sunlight from warming the Earth as it did before, causing temperatures to dip and affecting just about everything from farming to tourism.

Aside from that, a destructive nuclear war wouldn't have too much of an effect on the weather. In fact, the weather would play a major role in determining where radioactive materials would disperse after the explosions—prevailing winds would sweep radiation away from the many grounds zero, resulting in the deaths of thousands (if not millions) of people from radiation poisoning or cancer.

On the upside—okay, there really isn't an upside. Aside from the fact that we survived the Cold War, when there were times that this scenario seemed almost likely, and hopefully most governments are smarter these days about not wanting to destroy the entire planet.

INDEX

Numbers refer to the item number. Unnumbered items are indexed by which numbered item they follow. So, *"following* 54" means find this information in the box that appears after the text numbered 54.

A

air pressure
  high- and low-pressure systems, 6
  highest recorded, *following* 45
  during hurricanes, *following* 162
  ridges and troughs, 6
  on surface analysis charts, 7
  warning signs of tornadoes, 105
air travel
  contrails, 210
  lightning and, 122
  in winter, 70, *following* 91
Alberta Clippers, 58, 78
alcohol, using to keep warm, *following* 22
altocumulus clouds, 13
altostratus clouds, 13
Andrew (hurricane), 163, 178
animals
  behavior during droughts, 196
  behavior of as storms approach, 117
  evacuating with pets before hurricanes, 162
  winter safety, 26
Apollo 17, 11
Arthur (hurricane), 178
automobiles
  clearing ice off, *following* 91
  clearing snow off, *following* 91
  cold temperatures, 25
  driving in blizzards, 69
  driving in heavy rain, 135
  driving in high winds, 134
  driving on black ice, 44
  driving on flooded roads, 138, 140, 175
  encountering fallen power lines, 136
  evacuating before hurricanes, 162
  getting out of mud, 148
  hydroplaning, 137
  lightning and, 127
  outrunning storm surges, 165
  surviving tornadoes, 104, 114
  surviving when snowbound, 38
  traction on ice, 49
  winter driving, 37, *following* 91
  winter preparedness kit, 37, 51
autumn. *See* fall

B

ball lightning, 120
balloons, 12
barometers, 6
birds, behavior of as storms approach, 117
blizzards. *See also* snow
  avoiding complacency, 68
  defined, 65
  driving in, 69
  staying oriented in, 67
blue icebergs, *following* 77
bolt from the blue, 120

C

Camille (hurricane), 163
camping
  flooding and, 151
  lightning and, 127
  rocket stoves, 64
  thunderstorms and, 118
  wilderness survival kits, 43
canyons, 192
Catarina (hurricane), 163
CC (cloud-to-cloud) lightning, 120
central dense overcast, 157
CG (cloud-to-ground) lightning, 120
Charley (hurricane), 178
cirrus clouds, 13
cloud seeding, 209
clouds
  associated with supercells, 93
  associated with tornadoes, 101, 105
  scud, 102
  types of, 13
cloud-to-cloud (CC) lightning, 120
cloud-to-ground (CG) lightning, 120
cold
  catching a cold from, *following* 66
  coldest recorded temperature, *following* 32
  cold-proofing shotguns, 42
  frostbite, 18, 22, 26
  frozen pipes, 25
  hypothermia, 33, 72
  licking cold metal, *following* 63
  protection from cold winds, 23
  running automobiles in, 25
cold fronts
  defined, 8
  wildfires and, 202

cone tornadoes, 115
conspiracy theories, 208–210, 213
contours, 5
contrails, 210
cryoseisms, 24
cumulonimbus clouds, 13, 93
cumulus clouds, 13

D

deformation zones, 57
dendritic snowflakes, 31
Dennis (hurricane), 178
derechos, 186
deserts
  finding water in, 191–192
  locations of, 190
  overview of, 189
dew point
  on SKEW-T charts, 29
  on surface analysis charts, 7
Doppler radar, 10, 95
downbursts, 132
droughts
  drought-proofing homes, 195
  Dust Bowl, *following* 195
  during El Niño and La Niña, 207
  fishing during, 197
  hunting during, 196
  planning for, 194
dry lightning, 120, 200
dry lines, 8
dry microbursts, 132
dual-polar radar, 95
Dust Bowl, *following* 195

E

ECMWF (European Centre for Medium-Range Weather Forecasts; Euro), 4
Edmund Fitzgerald (ship), 71
El Niño
  conditions during, 207
  La Niña coming after, *following* 205
  overview of, 206
emergency preparedness. *See also names of specific types of emergency conditions*
  kits for, 15
  preparing home, 16
Environment Canada, 14
erosion

DENNIS MERSEREAU

Dennis Mersereau is an avid weather geek who fell in love with the weather before he could talk. Raised in northern Virginia and a graduate of the University of South Alabama, he grew up around nature's temper tantrums and is fond of extreme weather of all sorts. A childhood full of blizzards and thunderstorms—as well as the tornado outbreak of April 27, 2011—were all formative in his love and respect for the weather and those who forecast it. He enjoys traveling, commercial aviation, making maps, and spending his days doing the most dangerous job in the world: blogging. He writes for the Washington Post's Capitol Weather Gang and blogs for the Daily Kos. He is the creator of Gawker's weather vertical, The Vane, where he keeps readers up to date on the big weather events of the day, as well as answering questions like "Why Can't the Weatherman Tell Me if It Will Rain at My House Today?".

ROBERT F. JAMES

Robert F. James is a U.S. Navy veteran who nearly killed himself on an endurance bicycle race through Death Valley, and survived to race it again...more than once. He now resides on a small homestead in the Santa Cruz Mountains of California. In addition to hunting and fishing, he's constantly adding to and expanding his hobby farm. Currently, he raises rabbits, chickens, and ducks, among other things, and is an avid gardener. In his spare time, he is a lecturer in the English Department of San Jose State University.

OUTDOOR LIFE

Since it was founded in 1898, *Outdoor Life* magazine has provided survival tips, wilderness skills, gear reports, and other essential information for hands-on outdoor enthusiasts. Each issue delivers the best advice in hunting, fishing, and other outdoor sports, as well as thrilling true-life tales, detailed gear reviews, insider hunting, shooting, and fishing hints, and much more to nearly 1 million readers. Its survival-themed web site also covers disaster preparedness and the skills you need to thrive anywhere from the backcountry to the urban jungles. Whatever the weather's like where you are, *Outdoor Life* has you covered.

ILLUSTRATION CREDITS

PHOTOGRAPHY CREDITS

weldon**owen**

President & Publisher Roger Shaw
Associate Publisher Mariah Bear
SVP, Sales & Marketing Amy Kaneko
Finance Director Philip Paulick
Project Editor Robert F. James
Editorial Assistant Ian Cannon
Creative Director Kelly Booth
Art Director William Mack
Illustration Coordinator Conor Buckley
Production Director Chris Hemesath
Production Mananger Michelle Duggan
Director of Enterprise Systems Shawn Macey
Imaging Manager Don Hill

Weldon Owen would also like to thank Katharine Moore for editorial assistance and Kevin Broccoli for the index.

Special thanks to Tanja Fransen, Acting Meteorologist in Charge at NOAA/National Weather Service in Glasgow, MT for her invaluable assistance in checking the manuscript.

DESIGN BY CAMERON + COMPANY
Art Director Iain R. Morris
Designer Suzi Hutsell

© 2015 Weldon Owen Inc.
1045 Sansome Street, #100
San Francisco, CA 94111
www.weldonowen.com

Outdoor Life and Weldon Owen are divisions of

BONNIER

Library of Congress Control Number
on file with the publisher

Flexicover edition: ISBN 13: 978-1-61628-953-9
Hardcover edition: ISBN 978-1-68188-020-4
10 9 8 7 6 5 4 3 2 1
2015 2016 2017 2018 2019
Printed in China by 1010 Printing International

OUTDOOR LIFE

Executive Vice President Eric Zinczenko
Publisher Gregory D. Gatto
Editorial Director Anthony Licata
Editor-in-Chief Andrew McKean
Executive Editor John Taranto
Managing Editor Jean McKenna
Senior Deputy Editor John B. Snow
Deputy Editor Gerry Bethge
Assistant Managing Editor Margaret M. Nussey
Assistant Editor Alex Robinson
Senior Administrative Assistant Maribel Martin
Design Director Sean Johnston
Deputy Art Director Pete Sucheski
Senior Associate Art Director Kim Gray
Associate Art Director James A. Walsh
Photography Director John Toolan
Photo Editor Justin Appenzeller
Production Manager Judith Weber
Digital Director Nate Matthews
Online Content Editor Alex Robinson
Online Producer Kurt Schulitz
Assistant Online Content Editor Martin Leung

2 Park Avenue
New York, NY 10016
www.outdoorlife.com